A
Life
at
Risk

RICK AVERY

with Tom Bleecker

Gilderoy
Publications
Menifee, California

Gilderoy Publications titles are available at quantity discounts for sales promotions, premiums, or fund raising. For information, contact Gilderoy Publications at Gilderoy@aol.com.

The authors of this book strongly suggest that the reader does not attempt any stunt described in this book. In the event that the reader uses any of the information in this book to attempt any of the stunts or other physical actions described in this book, which is the reader's constitutional right, the authors and the publisher assume no responsibility for the reader's actions.

Library of Congress Cataloging-in-Publication Data

Avery, Rick 1947-
A Life at Risk, Rick Avery with Tom Bleecker
p.cm.
ISBN 978-0-6927250-7-8 (trade paper)
Avery, Rick 1947- 2. Hollywood stuntman—Hands of Stone—Policemen—Martial Arts—biography. I. Bleecker, Tom. II. Title.

First printing, May 2016

The paper used in this publication meets the minimum requirements of the American National Standard for Information Sciences—Performance of Paper for Printed Library Materials, ANSI Z39.48-1984. Printed in the United States of America

Designed by: Kurt Wahlner, www.wahlner.com

To **Alan Gibbs**, the
greatest stuntman ever and
the most charismatic man's
man I have ever known.
For your unselfish help and
kindness, without which
my career in stunts would
not have excelled or this
book been written, I shall be
eternally grateful.

Table of Contents

The Cover

1992, on the set of *Innocent Blood*. Pittsburg, 20 degrees, 3 a.m. "Rick, we're ready" comes over the PA. I put on dry fire retardant Nomex underwear, Nomex socks. I'm calm, as I've been here before. The pressure of a big stunt, lots of money being spent by production to get this accomplished. Film means your mistake, if made, will be captured for all to see. Time to step up and sell out. Go big or go home! Two safety stuntmen, Richard Epper and Monty Cox, help me get dressed—wet, fire gel soaked Nomex underwear come out of an ice chest and goes over the dry. Two layers. Then the fire suit over it all, followed by flame retardant wardrobe. I'm doubling actor Robert Loggia, who an hour earlier was serenading the crew with a beautiful operatic voice between takes from the roof of a five-story building. The oxygen bottle is tied to my calf and a small tube of air sent up through my collar. The multi camera crew awaits me on set as we walk out. The smell of the gel reminds me of past burns and what can be easy money.

But there are permanently scarred stuntmen in Hollywood who are a testament to this stunt going bad from just a few seconds of misjudgment. A flame retardant prosthetic mask that matches Robert Loggia's face is slipped over my head. I'm on the bottle . . . 2 minutes of air . . . My safety crew starts painting my body with highly-flammable contact cement . . . the crew is silent . . . this kind of stunt always freaks them out. Monty Cox tells the director we're ready . . . Yep, heart starts pumping . . . glass over eyes fogs up . . . visualize your action in your mind, Rick . . . heart now racing . . . good . . . adrenaline slows decisions down . . . protects . . . just don't let it get out of control . . . that's experience . . . never let it get out of control . . . "Roll cameras," the director yells . . . multiple cameras roll and sound respond "Speed!" Then—"ACTION!" My guys light me up . . . I start walking forward . . . Fully engulfed in flames ten feet high . . . I'm a vampire on fire . . . I have to look calm as I walk because it doesn't hurt Robert Loggia,

who is giving a speech over the fire, so I have to mimic like I'm talking . . . Keep walking . . . at first no heat . . . then the warmth comes . . . time to keep attentive . . . if you wait until it gets hot, it's too late . . . burned . . . Experience . . . not too soon, not too late . . . Okay, it's time . . . I fall to my knees, which is the signal for my safety crew to move in and put me out . . . "CUT!" . . . extinguishers put me out. I stand . . . the mask is removed to a standing ovation from the crew . . . calm and relief. Hero.

To explain how I ended up allowing myself to be set on fire, I need to start at the beginning . . .

Chapter 1:

Childhood

My earliest memories are of a circle of women with powdered makeup and perfectly styled hairstyles of the day, gleaming white teeth, and red lipstick. Some are smoking and some are wearing white gloves. They're staring down at me with admiration and glee. I lie there giggling from my baby carriage, as kisses rain down on me.

My first 13 years of life were spent joyously in New York City's East Bronx during the '50s when good and evil were clearly defined by parents, teachers, and the media. Good guys wore white and bad guys wore black. Life was simple, and I felt protected and secure.

I come from working class grit. Each generation before me worked hard and passed their earnings and learned skills onto the next generation.

My paternal family were all laborers who lived in England in the early 1700s. My grandfather, Kenneth Leo Avery, was a WWI veteran who served in France with the 7th infantry division. He was a

Me, Pop, and Grandma Schoen.

teamster who married an Italian lady named Ida Sala. Both of them died at an early age after having four children—my father Edward, Charlie, Rosemarie, and Virginia.

Ida's sister, Rose, stepped in and raised the orphaned children with her husband, Charles Mercandino. Charles and Rose, whom we called "Auntie" and "Uncle" lived in Peekskill, New York. Charles was a stone mason who helped to build West Point in West Point, New York, and Union Station in Washington, D.C. He was still building stone walls into his 80s and lived to be over 100 years of age. Including her sister's four orphaned children, Auntie raised a total of 25 foster children entirely on her husband's wages. For her efforts, she was awarded a humanitarian award in Westchester, New York.

My maternal grandfather, William Schoen, was a Russian Jew who, along with his brothers and sisters, fled Latvia from the Cossacks in the early 1900s. When he arrived at New York's Ellis Island, he spoke no English, had five dollars, a suitcase, and a mandolin. A short, stocky man with a broad chest, "Pop," as we called him, worked menial jobs until he earned a degree in mechanical engineering from Columbia College.

My mother Renee was William Schoen's only child. After WWII, she married my father Edward, who was a sailor on the destroyer U.S.S. *Edison* that saw action in the North Atlantic. He bore a scar on his face, but would never divulge how he got it. With the help of Pop, my father later procured a job as a mechanical engineer.

My parents had four children. I'm the eldest, followed by my brother Keith, and then my two identical twin sisters. Mom was kept busy in a time when baby bottles and rubber nipples needed to be boiled and diapers were hand washed. By the time the twins came, Mom told my brother and me to "go play outside," just to get us out of her hair.

I attended elementary school (PS 97) and Frank D. Whalen Junior High School (PS 135). For me, "the neighborhood," as it was defined in New York City life, amounted to a small, four square block

Mom and Dad.

Grammar school class, middle row far right.

area that consisted mainly of Italians and Jews. The kids in my neighborhood rarely ventured outside of this comfortable area.

Although no one knew at the time, many of the children who played together in East Bronx were destined to find fame and fortune in Hollywood, including Jennifer Lopez, James Caan, Lauren Bacall, Rob Reiner, Tony Curtis, Billy Joel, and Vin Scully.

My childhood happened before computers, the Internet, and video games of any kind. When I came home from school, I went outside and played. My mother didn't have to check up on me because the neighborhood mothers were responsible for all the kids, or at least they kept an eye on our comings and goings. We were a prime example of "it takes a village to raise a kid." This was a time when any parent could discipline any kid (or feed him or use him to carry groceries) and nobody—not even the kid—thought a thing of it.

My childhood was living on the stoop. I played mush ball, stickball, handball, and stoopball until the last streetlight came on. With wonderment, throughout the evening, I captured fireflies in a glass jar and poked holes in the jar's top to allow them to breathe. Yes, it was dumb, but caring.

On hot summer days, we'd run through the sprinklers and quench our thirst with a glass of Kool Aid or a swig from the garden hose. My bike was my horse that I rode everywhere. Because I had attached baseball cards to my bike's frame with wooden clothespins, I could be heard from a block away. Back then, kids actually got tired from playing.

We didn't have pagers and cellphones. When dinnertime came, my mother would stand on the front porch and scream, "Ricky! Dinner! Ricky, c'mon! Supper's on the table!" and I'd come running. Throughout the neighborhood there were similar calls from mothers around the dinner hour.

Our brownstone house at 2506 Morgan Avenue had three floors. The basement level, which was above ground; the first floor where the living room and kitchen were; and the second floor where the bedrooms were located. At first, we didn't have a refrigerator. An iceman, wearing a leather apron, would climb the stairs with a 50-pound block of ice thrown over his back to put in our "icebox."

After we got our first television around the time I was four, watching TV was a welcomed source of family entertainment. We would all gather around it religiously to watch *The Wonderful World of Disney* and *The Ed Sullivan Show*. Whenever time allowed, I could be found sitting in front of the tube, eating Oreo cookies and watching *Looney Tunes*. Of course, I watched *The Mickey Mouse Club* every day and, like every boy in my generation, fell in love with Annette Funicello.

Dad would leave the house early in the morning, leaving mom with the household duties and return shortly before dinnertime. He worked throughout his life at American Machine and Foundry (AMF), which was once the largest manufacturer of recreational equipment in the United States.

2506 Morgan Avenue.

Because my mother was a college graduate and had a Russian-Jewish work ethic, running the household wasn't enough. To supplement our income, she took part-time work as a door-to-door saleswoman for the Avon Company selling cosmetics.

My parents instilled their strong work ethic in me, and as a result I starting working when I was 11 years old. Besides selling comic books and holiday greeting cards door-to-door, I had a paper route and picked up a few dollars mowing lawns and cashing in empty soda bottles for the deposit money.

Back then, a little money bought a lot. I spent most of it on ten-cent comic books and baseball cards that came five in a pack along with a flat piece of pink bubble gum that was coated with powdered sugar. For ten cents, I could buy a chocolate egg cream or some potato chips.

Most of my endeavors, however, lost money. Thankfully, I had a security blanket in my mother and grandparents, who would pay for the stuff I didn't sell. Throughout their lifetimes, they always had my skinny back.

At times, winter snow fell heavily in New York. There were two big hills around the corner from my house, and when the cars weren't passing on the road, my heavily-jacketed friends and I would carelessly race our sleds down those hills. To get back to the top of the hills, we'd slip behind a passing car that was trying to gain traction up the hill, and grab onto their rear bumpers. Lying prone on our sleds, we'd fight exhaust fumes as the unknowing driver dangerously towed us back to the top.

In the summer, I'd awaken to the crisp, fresh air drifting in my open window and the sounds of the Bronx—honking horns, the milkman's clinking bottles, the clanging of trash can lids, and the Italian fruit and vegetable truck with its driver yelling, "Fresha fruita!" These were the times when practically every delivery service came to the house, including the family doctor carrying his small black bag with those scary big needles.

During the week, I attended day camp that offered supervised activities for kids, and then on weekends my family drove to neighboring Peekskill where Auntie and Uncle Mercandino owned a home. Peekskill is situated along the east side of the Hudson River, across from Jones Point. Its steep hills create an amphitheater for views of the Hudson and the surrounding green hills. Most houses then were Victorians and small ranches.

On arrival, the adults and children were always separated. While my parents and the Mercandinos talked about grown up things, I ran into the countryside with the other kids to pick berries, play Army, climb ropes and swing from trees, and fish in the creek from an old broken bridge that spanned it.

We'd often go to nearby Lakeland Acres that had a huge man-made lake. The entry was sand, but after ten feet, the sand turned to mud with clusters of rocks covered with slimy algae. I'd swim in that lake for hours, never tiring of the fun.

My dad was a great golfer and owned a golfing range in Peek-skill. The demands of four kids prevented him from pursing his dream of turning professional. To this day, when I see a bucket of golf balls, a warm feeling comes over me from the memories of sitting on the black tee off mats playing with buckets of balls. I'd watch my dad's perfect form while he practiced his golf shots. His swing was so powerful that he could drive the ball more than 300 yards, and his aim was so precise that he could hit the moving caged cart picking up balls on the range. I remember this with pride, but also a feeling of melancholy because he was never able to make his dream come true.

When we were in Peekskill, I was forced to go to church with my aunt and uncle, who were Roman Catholics. I'd put on a suit and tie and, along with my brother and sisters, be dragged to church. I still remember those hard straight-backed pew benches and being bored to tears by lackluster sermons that seemed to go on forever.

Lakeland Acres.

Above, me sitting on the golf mat; right, dad's golf swing.

My parents were liberal when it came to religion. My mother was Jewish and my father, although raised by devout Catholics, was an atheist. When I turned 12, and because my grandparents were both Jewish and Catholic, I was given the choice of becoming a Catholic or a Jew. I hardly knew which one to pick. Ironically, the deciding factor was when I was told that I'd make more money at a bar mitzvah, which resulted in my becoming a Jew. Looking back, the truth is that, although I was made to feel like I was given a choice, having a Jewish mother dictated I was Jewish.

Because we had six family members, there was often a birthday celebration at home, but nothing topped Christmas. My dad would stay up all night putting the train set together and helping Mom wrap presents. Best of all, there was always a "big present" that was either opened or appeared from out of nowhere when all the other presents had been opened. I would eagerly sit beside the tree, waiting for that big present because I knew that my mother's philosophy raising four

Mom in party mode.

kids was that whatever her children wanted, she was going to get it. There was nothing she wouldn't sacrifice for them.

The majority of my parents' generation—both men and women—drank alcohol and smoked cigarettes and loved a good party. One memorable social gathering that stands out in my mind was when I was six years old, my parents hosted a New Year's Eve party at our house. When the party was in full swing, I was practically choking on the smell of alcohol and cigarette smoke, as the group loudly bellowed out, "Roll me over in the clover, Roll me over, Lay me down and do it again."

In the 1950s, it was common for a man come home from work, play Frank Sinatra on the hi-fi, and have a drink before dinner. And when going out with friends, a boilermaker or beer before dinner was standard. My dad was more than a social drinker. I think he endured considerable stress at work and used alcohol to wind down in the evenings. In the morning, I often saw him chug down a large glass of milk before leaving for work. In retrospect, I've wondered if his gulping a glass of milk in the morning was because he had a stomach ulcer.

On weekends, around the time I was eight years old, he would sometimes send me two blocks to Nat's Italian Delicatessen to get him a six pack of Schlitz beer. I'd give Nat the money, and he'd hand me the beer in a paper bag and say, "Now make sure nobody sees you." I'd return home with the beer. I never knew why Nat was so cautious. No one, including the police, would have cared about my going to the store to buy beer for my father.

One time I went to Nat's with my younger brother Keith. I was 12 at the time. I waited outside while he went into the deli. I was leaning against the wall of the building when he suddenly came running from the store and took off down the street. Moments later, Nat raced outside in his apron and took off after him, yelling expletives in Italian. Upon seeing Nat's reddened face, I took off running, as well.

An hour later, a cop appeared at our house and informed my mother that Nat was claiming that he saw Keith stuffing items in his pockets, and that when Nat confronted Keith, my brother took off running (all true, Keith admits today). Nevertheless, Nat wanted to talk to Keith—and me. Even though I hadn't done anything, I still got in trouble because Nat planted the seed in the cop's ear that I was the ringleader and lookout.

My brother and I returned to Nat's Deli and sat before Nat, who smiled and excitedly rubbed his hands together, as he spoke with a strong Italian accent. "Okay, you gotta caught stealing froma me," he said. "So what're you going to do about it?" We didn't have any idea, but he did. "Imma gonna talka to your dad," Nat continued. "I think a fair solution isa for you two boys to worka for me and worka this offa."

My brother and I worked for Nat part-time for two full weeks. From day one, he trusted us with his money and taught us how to use the cash register. When customer traffic was slow, we stacked shelves and replenished the refrigerated deli trays. Surprisingly, it was a fun experience. On our lunch break, Nat, who was pleased with our work, made us the biggest hero sandwich of anything we wanted, plus a soda and chips. This was one of many examples of the neighborhood taking care of its own children by teaching them a lesson in the right way.

At school, sociology and geography class teachers were pushing an outward reach by having students communicate with the rest of the world. As a result, around the age of 12, I became one of thousands of Pen pals spread throughout many countries. This was perhaps the first rudimentary Facebook. I began exchanging letters with people who lived in the United States and abroad. I was a shy kid around people I didn't know, and so Pen pals was a way that I could make friends without a face-to-face meeting.

About a year later, I became a ham radio operator, which started as a hobby. I installed an antenna on our roof and aimed it across the Atlantic Ocean. Eventually, I was able to pick up "Radio Free

Nat's Deli.

Europe" and other foreign stations and communicated with English speaking people in other countries.

Although my parents and grade school teachers tried to shield me from negative world news, I was able to pick up information by eavesdropping on my parents' conversations, as well as what I heard over my ham radio. It wasn't good. Although WWII had ended, the political differences between the leaders of the Free World and the Soviet Union had in no way subsided. What had been a "hot war" was being continued as a "Cold War." Besides the ongoing Korean War, both the United States and the Soviet Union were developing nuclear warheads at an alarming rate. Amid the growing fear that this Cold War would trigger WWIII and that the Soviet Union would launch intercontinental ballistic missiles aimed at America, I tried my best to be optimistic.

There was a much greater positive side of my life. My family was always supportive. I got along famously with my brother, and even danced with my sisters. In the evening, I was excited when I heard the front door open and my mother call out, "Daddy's home." Unfortunately, my dad wasn't anywhere near as engaged. He would often eat dinner in relative silence, and then retire to the living room to watch television. To say that he was emotionally distant would be a fair statement.

My father never came into my room at night to kiss me goodnight on the forehead or tell me bedtime stories like my mother did. The one endearing moment that I remember of my father, however, was when we were driving home one Sunday night from Peekskill. I had fallen asleep on the backseat, and when we arrived at our house, he carried me up the stairs to my bedroom. Halfway up, I faked still being asleep. I remember this as being a special, warm moment. Being in my father's arms was meaningful to me then, and it still is to this day because it was so rare.

As time passed, my dad fell into a rut at work, became depressed, and increased his drinking. As a result, there were times when his temper would flare. One weekend while we were driving to Peekskill, he got upset with me and my brother who were playing loudly in the back seat. "You kids shut up back there or I'll smack you!" he yelled. "Just make yourselves small!" My dad wasn't physically abusive, and in fact he never hit us. But the threat was enough, and we were too fast in retreat. It was his tone that was upsetting to me because I wanted to please him and not be a problem in his life.

I rarely spent time with my father. We sometimes silently watched

television together. Throughout the four years that I played Little League baseball, he came to only one of my games. The best time I remember with him was the day he took me to watch the New York Yankees play at Yankee Stadium. I was excited seeing Mickey Mantle play because I had a dozen of his baseball cards. What a thrill it was to be at the ballpark that was home to many of the greatest baseball players, including (along with Mickey Mantle) Babe Ruth, Lou Gehrig, Joe DiMaggio, Whitey Ford, and Yogi Berra.

My father wasn't a part of my early childhood because he was working all the time trying to support a wife and four children. Like most kids back then, my image of a father was what I saw on the TV show *Father Knows Best*. My dad came home still wearing a suit and tie. I suppose I didn't notice the lack of a father/son relationship because I was into my friends.

Around the time I turned 12 years of age, I began to have a strong feeling of inadequacy. The first time I recall feeling this way was when I was playing stickball with the neighborhood kids, and when

Opposite, with my brother and twin sisters. Right, as the catcher on the Farenga Brothers Astor Little League.

we'd choose up sides, I was the last one picked. This repeated itself in every arena where kids were being chosen.

This condition of being not enough or good enough was compounded whenever I got around girls. Around that same time, I was at my house with a group of boys and girls. My mother was present, and we were all in the living room and decided to play the age-old kids' game "Spin the Bottle." One of the girls spun the bottle, and when it landed on me, she and all her girlfriends simultaneously squealed,

"Eeewwww!" as they scrunched up their faces. While it was true that I was a pimply faced kid, from the pictures I've looked at dating back to that time, I was a fairly good looking lad, although at the time my self-image was that I was plain looking, at best.

Physical fights in my neighborhood were rare. I was riding my bicycle through the schoolyard one afternoon and somebody took a stickball bat and threw it like a spear into my front wheel and flipped me over.

There were gangs around East Bronx, although thankfully not in my four square block neighborhood. The Ragnos family were some mean Italian guys. On the few occasions that I ran across these guys, they stood up for me and said, "Leave the kid alone!" They most likely did this because I resembled a Biafra victim. I was pigeon-chested and would at least once a month would ask my Auntie Mercandino, "How do I get rid of the bones in my back, Auntie?"

Her answer to my question was always the same. "Eat more pasta!"

"Uncle Charles" Mercandino 100 years plus.

Uncle Charles had a chicken coop on his property in Peekskill. He would grab fresh eggs and a chicken, which he would swing until its neck was broken, and then deliver them to Auntie. She would de-feather the chicken, and if we were bothering her, she would call us to the sink where she would pop out the chicken's eyes. This never failed to get us bolting from her kitchen, screaming.

There was one neighborhood bully named Billy Kowalski, who threatened to punch me in the arm every day on my way to school. "Give me your lunch money," he'd snarl, "or I'm going to punch you in the arm!" He never punched me in the face, thank God, probably because I was a frail little guy and he didn't want to look like the bully that he was. As a footnote, years later when I visited the "block," I was told by the owner of the candy store that Billy had been killed in prison.

I got in only one real fight as a kid and was losing badly when a kindhearted woman saved me. Initially, I thought I could get out of the fight by screaming louder at the kid, which resulted in him beating the crap out of me until that woman came to my rescue.

Although Dad was often at work, I felt that if anything threatened us, he could take care of it. I always saw him as a huge man, but the fact was he stood only 5'6" and for most of his life was lean.

One afternoon, the next door neighbor was upset with my eight-year-old brother playing in the neighbor's yard. In his outlandish rage, he lifted my brother above his head and threatened to throw him down on the ground. My dad learned about this when he got home that night. Minutes later, the entire block was standing outside the neighbor's house, witnessing my dad calling the man out. "You ever put your hands on my kids again, I'll beat your ass." Rightfully so, the guy feared for his life and stayed barricaded in his house. I was proud of my dad that day. It confirmed why I felt secure knowing he would never allow anything bad to happen to us.

The stark reality, however, was that my dad wasn't around 24/7, and I was too light to fight and too thin to win—and I certainly had zero warrior's spirit. Because of this and my general frailty, I was afraid of going to Columbus High School, which was where I was headed. That school was a tough place, and just its reputation was enough to scare me to death. Once I got to the high school level, all kinds of different neighborhoods would enter my sphere, and there were plenty of bad neighborhoods in other parts of the Bronx.

In a sheer stroke of good fortune, it was the time of the Cold War between the United States and the Soviet Union that saved me. I had witnessed degrees of tension when my school teachers began instructing students on how to do "drop drills" (aka "duck and cover"), which essentially had the entire classroom diving under our desks and covering our heads from potentially falling debris resulting from a nuclear explosion. This all had to do with the escalating threat of the Soviet Union's nuclear power.

It was around this time that my father's company, which was once a major diversified manufacturer of bowling paraphernalia and tennis rackets, landed a government contract to build nuclear reactors and missile launching silos for the Titan and Atlas ICBMs. Because of this, the company told my father that he was being transferred to Colorado.

This was perfectly fine with me because I'd been studying my school's geography book and making a note of how far New York was from Moscow. Clearly, I would be much safer in Colorado, which was another 1,500 miles away from the Soviet Union missile sites and, even better, 1,500 miles away from Columbus High School!

Chapter 2:

The Trek West

We packed up the small, blue Falcon station wagon full of two adults, four kids, and a roof rack full of luggage and made the trek to Aurora, Colorado, near Denver. Dad leased a small, three-bedroom apartment next door to a drive in theater that we could watch out of our bedroom windows, which also had a view of the spectacular snow-capped Rocky Mountains.

Dad got into cowboy life almost immediately. He bought a cowboy hat, boots, and an assortment of guns. The guns proved to be an unwise act for Dad, as he was a boiler man in the Navy, not an infantryman. One night, he was sitting at the kitchen table, cleaning his new 30-30 rifle when it suddenly it went off! We were shocked! We looked up at the ceiling and saw a hole in it. My dad ran to our upstairs neighbor, who was having his dinner at his kitchen table when the bullet came up through the floor, grazing his cheek. He was pissed, to say the least. Dad eventually had to go to court, and it was ruled an accident.

Our lifestyle quickly improved. AMF gave Dad a new 1959 red and white Chevy Impala for a company car, which as the first automobile he ever owned that had power steering and air conditioning. Best of all, he was earning more money and wore a smile from ear-to-ear.

Our family would go on a driving adventure every weekend. We panned for gold in Colorado Springs, drove up the narrow winding roads of Pike's Peak, and visited the Air Force Academy. Practically every weekend, we experienced the wonder and beauty of Colorado.

Dad was finally doing the things he wanted to do. He was happy when he and his boys rented local horses to ride. I always rode a quarter horse named Blackjack. The horses were old, worn out nags that needed prodding to leave the stable. But the second they were turned around, they suddenly became prime races horses whose mouths were as insensitive to their bits as their ribs were to boot heels. I held on for dear life the first few times, but as the months passed, we got pretty good galloping across the green hills and valleys.

Besides horseback riding, my father took the whole family shooting. We'd go out and try shooting fixed targets, as well as magpies from trees. Although we did all right with the targets, to the magpies' delight, we never got close, as they looked down laughing from above.

Meanwhile, I was settling in nicely at Aurora Central High School. I was still small in stature, but tried out for the football team. All I had to do was show up and I was given a helmet and jersey. Because the coaches put me on a weight program, I gained muscle.

I played cornerback for the junior varsity squad. One assignment was to stop or contain the end around run. I'd see a guard or tackle coming my way, leading a running back, and the whole group of them would run over me. Although I had no idea at the time, this was the first taste of what would become my life's profession.

Originally, I wanted to try out as an end because that's where all the glory—and thus the validation—was. The quarterback touchdown pass to the end was a surefire way to get the crowd leaping to their feet and cheering uncontrollably. The problem was my hands were small, and so I could rarely hold onto the football. The good news was the coach saw that I was fast enough to get to the ball, so he put me on defense where I alternated playing cornerback and outside linebacker. The result, however, was pretty much the same. I got to the ball just in time to get my ass whooped.

The riding and shooting added to my bonding with Dad. Then one day, he announced that he and his friends from work were going on a weekend hunt and invited me to go along. I was ecstatic by what I felt would be some sort of African safari. Best of all, I was going with my father and the "big guys." This had the feel of a young boy's rite of passage. I was 14 at the time. I didn't have an expectation of what we would do, just that I was going out with the guys and we were bringing our guns. Just to be a part of that was beyond cool.

We awoke early because we were traveling out of state. One of my father's friends had an old 1948 Buick that we drove 250 miles from Aurora into Wyoming to hunt for antelope. We didn't find any antelope. All we found was freezing cold, and no one was dressed right. We had shotguns, 30-30 rifles, and handguns, but all we did was drive across the plains of Wyoming in a 1948 Buick that needed shocks and springs. It was tragically comical and something that belonged in a movie like *Blazing Saddles*.

At the end of the great safari, we hadn't killed anything. Then on our last day as the sun was setting, we saw a herd of antelope running across the plains. Glory Halleluiah! Blessed be! These stupid guys decided they were going to chase down those antelope and shoot them. Well, it's impossible to chase down antelope in a dilapidated 1948 Buick bouncing across the prairie. It was ridiculous. It was like watching Bill Murray and Joe Pesci going hunting.

Totally humiliated, my dad and his friends finally ground that tired old Buick to a bumpy stop and bailed out. Twenty minutes later, trudging over the icy ground, they managed to find a big jack rabbit and shot it. The rabbit wasn't killed. It was only wounded, and it was screaming. That animal was morbidly terrified. I had a .22 rifle, and my dad told me to kill that rabbit. I couldn't do it. I stood in front of that animal that was trying to hide in a bush as it bled from several bullet holes, and I simply couldn't shoot it.

Finally, one of my dad's friends stepped on the rabbit and broke its neck. It was sad. I hated seeing it and being any part of it. We had tortured a totally defenseless rabbit. We couldn't even eat him, anyway. It was just shooting for shooting and hunting for hunting.

The reality of what I'd been a part of caused me to feel ashamed. At the end of the trip, whatever initial glory there was from going out with these guys was completely gone. All I did was go out with a bunch of daydreamers and acted stupid. None of us were qualified hunters. We didn't even have a plan. In the end, all we had was a dead jack rabbit that we left out on the prairie. This single event had an impact on me from that day forward. I kept those feelings to myself.

Six months after our failed hunting trip, I arrived home from school and instantly sensed that there was grieving going on in our house. Something was drawing the energy from the room. I moved slowly to the entrance to the living room where I saw my dad sitting on the couch, wearing his bathrobe and being consoled by my mother and a group of friends.

From early childhood, I'd been taught to stay out of "adult matters," and so I eavesdropped, not being able to discern what was being said besides condolences, and went to the bathroom. To my horror, the laundry hamper was filled with the clothes my father had been wearing. They were streaked with blood and there were bits of human skin and bone covering the fabric.

I later learned was there had been a catastrophic accident at work. One of the gigantic 58-ton doors of a Titan missile launching silo had accidently disengaged itself and slammed down on a crew of workers. The falling door, made of steel and concrete, cut one man's body in half, while smashing and mangling dozens of others, the remains of which were strewn over a 500 square-foot area. Five men were killed and eight others were seriously injured. My dad was there when it happened. He soon returned to drinking, undoubtedly suffering from survivor's remorse that resulted in him constantly asking himself, "Why did I survive and they didn't?"

After one year, my father's company transferred him to Southern California, most likely to get him away from the horrible accident site. Once again, the old Falcon station wagon trudged cross country as we played all the road trips games that kids play to pass the time. We put state line and historical site decals on the car's side windows, ate at burger stands and chain restaurants, and stayed at a different, inexpensive motel every night.

The weather was warm and breezy as we drove along the Holly-wood Freeway, and for the first time I saw swaying palm trees. I kept staring out the car's windows, mesmerized, convinced that I'd eventually see a movie star sitting behind the wheel of a gleaming Cadillac convertible.

Rolling out from the glitz and glimmer of Hollywood and Beverly Hills, we continued driving north for another hour. Santa Barbara is situated on a south-facing section of Pacific coastline (the longest such section on the West Coast of the United States). It lies between the steeply rising Santa Ynez Mountains and the Pacific Ocean. The climate is often described as Mediterranean, and the city has for years been promoted as the American Riviera.

Our family moved to Ladera Street on the lower west side in a small apartment until my parents could find a suitable house. All the kids were crammed into one room, sleeping on two sets of bunkbeds. Our temporary living conditions were one step above our prior week of motel living. During the 1960s, a man like my father, who made an average living, could raise his family of four kids in a comfortable manner. The American Dream was still a reality.

I spent three years at San Marcos High School where I developed a deep love of music and the performing arts. I played trumpet in the school's band and its award-winning orchestra, as well as in the marching band and jazz band. In addition, I sang in the barbershop quartet and three musicals: Rogers and Hammerstein's *The Flower Drum Song* and *Oklahoma*, and Meredith Willson's *The Music Man*. I also sang a cappella in the school's choir, and played guitar singing in a folk group called "The Nameless Nine."

I continued to be shy, especially around girls, and rarely dated. Although Dick Clark's rock 'n' roll era was in full swing, I didn't attend any of the sock hops or parties and didn't frequent the soda shops and drive-in movies. Besides one or two male friends, I remained a loner.

The first real challenge that required my seeing something through was when I was a member of the high school wrestling team. There's a closeness among wrestlers because they're intimate with each other. Some believe that wrestling is the toughest sport in the world because wrestlers use 100 percent of their bodies 100 percent of the time.

My team's first match was in Simi, California. I had developed somewhat from that skinny East Bronx kid with the pigeon chest. I wrestled at a whopping 123 pounds, and the guy I was set to wrestle was an Asian guy with arms the size of an old lady. My teammates slapped me on the back and assured me I'd pin this pencil neck in a matter of seconds, with which I wholeheartedly agreed.

My buddies were right. The match ended in a matter of seconds when the guy had my pencil neck pinned with my face in the mat. If that wasn't bad enough, I lost my next match in almost the same record time. The entire experience was monumentally embarrassing.

Coach Mangus chewed me out in front of the entire wrestling team, calling me a quitter. To me, his tirade was a form of bullying.

While I understood that he was trying to light a fire under me, I didn't agree with his method. Regardless, the ball was in my court. Either I fell by the wayside in a heap of stones or told myself, "Okay, I'm putting on my big boy pants and I'm going to fix this." This embarrassing method of motivation works with some and causes others to quit. It worked with me. Maybe the coach knew it would.

Over the next six weeks, I redoubled my weightlifting and cardiovascular workouts. My dedication and resolve paid off because when I fought a rematch with that Asian wrestler, I pinned him in 13 seconds. And although the wrestler from Simi, who beat me the first time, won our rematch, I fought hard throughout the duration of the match.

That day marked a turning point in my life because I no longer had "quit" in me. As long as I gave my full effort—and left it on the mat—even if I lost, I was a winner. That year I lettered in wrestling. It was a proud moment for me, although I was disappointed that my father, because of his heavy work schedule, wasn't able to watch any of my matches with many of the other fathers.

After the accident in Colorado, the depression that plagued my father when we lived in East Bronx returned. The week of our joyous and adventurous cross country drive from Colorado to California was gone, once again to be replaced by his survivor's remorse. He drank trying to replace the pain, only to gain weight to 180 lbs. and a beer belly.

Because of his work, he had his ear to the ground regarding the relations between the United States and the Soviet Union. This came to a head when on October 22, 1962, after reviewing photographic evidence, President John F. Kennedy informed the world that the Soviet Union was building secret missile bases in Cuba, just 90 miles off the shores of Florida.

In a TV address, President Kennedy notified Americans about his decision to enact a naval blockade around Cuba, and made it clear the U.S. was prepared to use military force if necessary to neutralize this perceived threat to national security. Following this news, many people feared the world was on the brink of nuclear war. Given that my father participated in building missile silos that housed America's ICBMs, I wondered whether he felt that if nuclear war broke out, he would be partially responsible for the deaths of tens of thousands of innocent victims.

Chapter 3:

My Work Ethic
Kicks In

W hen I turned 15, I worked for a few weeks picking lemons
for Sunkist Growers. The $1.89 per hour wasn't convinc-
ing enough to stay more than a few weeks for the tough,
dirty, laborious job. The experience taught me two things—one, that
to this day I have a tremendous respect for the countless number of
people who work tirelessly in California and Arizona's produce fields
and, two, that I needed to find another line of work if I intended to
make anything of myself.

A week later, I walked into the cramped office of the Red Horse
Mobil Gas Station. I had absolutely no experience working at a gas
station, so I was amazed and delighted when the owner, whose name
was Fred, hired me at minimum wage. In a friendly and relaxed demeanor, he said, "When there's work to be done, they'll be work to be
done, and when there's no work, feel free to nap here in the office."

This was full service station that, besides offering gas, had two
mechanic's bays. Attendants pumped gas, checked the oil and tire

pressures, and cleaned the windows—all with a friendly smile. The station even provided ice blocks for campers. A thin black rubber tube stretched across the entry lanes, and when a car pulled up to the pumps, it ran over that tube, triggering a "ding, ding" in the office.

Fred was such a great boss that when he went on vacation, one of the other grease monkeys and I painted the entire station. Fred was the first man who took an interest in me and, in his line of work, taught me everything from fixing a flat tire to repairing engines.

Far more important than teaching me, Fred validated my work. Best of all, he made good on his initial promise of napping in his office when there was no work. On more than one occasion when there was no business, we both dozed off in the office. There we were, the two of us sound asleep behind our desks, only to be awakened 20 minutes later by the office bell's "ding-ding!"

After I'd been working at that Mobil station for six months, I arrived home one day to find a 1953 Ford parked in our driveway. I'd never seen the car before, and when I asked my dad about it, he tossed me the keys and said, "You've earned it." I later found out that he'd spent $400 on that car, which was the entire paycheck he made in one month. Although he never verbally validated my work at that gas station, giving me that car told me that he was watching. Strangely enough, my father giving me that car is one of the few things I remember about him in all the time we spent in Santa Barbara.

My incentive tripled when my father gave me that car because I wanted to please him even more. Because of the good work I'd done at Fred's station, the station owner next door offered me work, which meant that I now had two jobs. A month later, that Ford allowed me to land a job at a third gas station in Isla Vista.

When my mom purchased her yellow 1964 Ford Falcon convertible, I drove it one weekend to watch the drag races. Thrilled to be at the races and suddenly eager to compete, I entered my mom's Falcon in the stock class and was as shocked as everyone else when the car

Drag racing my Mustang.

raced across the finish line looking like Big Bird and took first place. When I arrived home that evening, I lied to my mom about how I'd won it. Had she known that I was drag racing her new Ford Falcon, she would have killed me.

Among my school peers, I made up for my shyness and lack of popularity by having cool cars and my ability to repair my friends' cars when they broke down or needed routine maintenance. While I didn't have a macho appearance and demeanor, my cars and the name I'd made for myself at the drag races helped considerably. I became "a car guy."

In addition to frequently attending the drag races in nearby Santa Maria and occasionally going to the Riverside Raceway, I was elected president of the local Channel City Competition Team that was known as the "CCC Team" (The CCC Team). This was my first attempt at a leadership position in my life.

It was a normal school day on November 22, 1963. A saddened voice came over the school loudspeakers. The principal was summoning all of the student body to meet at the outside Greek theater. Once assembled, we were told that President John F. Kennedy had been assassinated in Dallas and that we should all go home.

I lived only a few blocks from San Marcos High School, and when I walked in the door, I found my mom crying. I thought, *well, this has affected her as much as the rest of us.* She approached me sobbing and put her head to my chest said, "Oh, Ricky, your father is sick."

I didn't quite understand.

"He has cancer," she said through her tears. "The doctors say there is nothing they can do about it. It's terminal."

I never saw it coming because my father appeared to be in relatively good health. He had known about his illness for some time, but kept the bad news from my mother.

Dad chose to remain at home rather than be admitted to a care facility. After a month, he spent all his time weak in bed. In his last days, my mother would sit hours by his side, and when she needed a break, would ask me to sit with him.

When a person is dying like this, their breathing is labored. It slows, sometimes to only two or three breaths a minute. I would sit at his bedside, terrified that each labored breath would be his last. Perhaps the years of drinking and smoking had taken its toll. He passed away a few months later from liver cancer. He was 40 years of age. I was 16.

Prior to this moment, I'd never been so upset. I can still remember watching the funeral procession with my father on T.V. and watching a three-year-old John Kennedy Jr. standing tall and proudly saluting his father's casket as it passed by. In the background, the chilling, monotonous drone of the drums. Bomp, bomp, bomp . . . bomp, bomp, bomp-bomp. The free and peaceful society as I knew it was falling apart, and it was profoundly scary. The world was changing radically. There would soon be more assassinations.

The day of his wake, I wasn't close to anyone present except my immediate family. I was uncomfortable and wanted to be anywhere but there. I walked to the open casket where he lay. My eyes filled with tears as I reached to touch his crossed hands on his chest. They were so cold and lifeless. I held the shock internally, wanting to jerk my hands away. Waiting until I wasn't noticed, I grabbed an unopened bottle of champagne and drove to San Marcos Pass and parked off the side of the road.

I got out of the car and sat on a large boulder, then uncorked the champagne and drank the whole bottle. When I was finished, I was stone sober. I glanced up at the Pacific Ocean where the setting sun cast its rays through clouds on a big ship that was sailing away from me toward the horizon. At that moment, I recalled my father having served in the Navy. An empty sadness overwhelmed me and a melancholy enveloped me as the ship disappeared. I knew I wasn't going to be able to explore maturity with him. All the weaknesses that he had, all the weaknesses I had, we were never going to be able to sit and talk about these things and have our relationship grow.

I took a deep breath and saluted the horizon, then set the empty bottle down on the roadway. Driving home, I wondered what I was going to do now that he was gone. Who would protect me? Who was going to teach me about life and how to become a man?

Mom grieved for a long time. Her "Sonny" (Dad's nickname) would never be coming home from a long day of work for dinner again. Because she had four children to raise and was now the sole breadwinner, she returned to college. Taking the most difficult path, she returned as a fulltime student to the renowned USC, driving to Los Angeles every Monday, staying in an apartment all week and returning to see us on the weekends. She eventually graduated with a degree specializing in cytotechnology. As a technician, she worked at

Left, Mom's first graduation; right, me and Scott Mitchell.

Cottage Hospital in Santa Barbara, examining cells for various diseases. Though small in stature, she stood heads above the rest. A strong woman. Grit . . . no quit . . . with grace.

❧ ❧ ❧

Scott Mitchell was one of my closest high school buddies. A football star, he was mature beyond his years. A macho guy and a man's man. He was a gifted athlete and someone I greatly admired. If I were to describe him in one word, it would be focused. In my mind, he was an icon.

One day, I was lazily lounging on the couch, as teenagers do, when he called on the phone asking me to go surfing with him. This was when the Beach Boys were big, as were Pendleton shirts, huarache sandals, and surfers putting lemon juice and peroxide in their hair. Skateboarding was just being invented. When I tried to make up some lame excuse, he chastised me for being lazy, which because of his status in my eyes, hurt me deeply. I would never, ever be lazy again in my life.

One freezing cold afternoon, he took me to a nearby surfing spot called "The Cove" that was adjacent to the University of California at Santa Barbara. We pulled into the parking lot and walked out to the edge of the cliffs and looked down at a dozen surfers wearing black rubber wetsuits and either sitting or riding their surfboards on five foot waves. To me, it was a sight to behold. The next day, I bought a surfboard and wetsuit and returned to The Cove and later "The Poles" and "The Point" nearby to begin my surfing safari.

Left, in the backyard with my first surfboard. Below, me surfing "The Cove."

I surfed for a couple of years and became addicted to it. I came home one day and my mother said I looked like a black person, my skin had become so dark from the sun. I knew all the surfer lingo and had the telltale surfer knots on my knees that were so advanced that they were actually holes. Back then, surfers paddled on their knees. Scott was relentless in keeping me active, as we became certified scuba divers together and went skydiving, making five jumps.

As I approached my senior year in high school, all my friends were talking about the girls and making considerable headway—and conquests. In sharp contrast, I continued to be the odd man out. It wasn't that I was a bad looking guy, or even a nerd, but that I didn't have any social skills around the young ladies. I had no playbook, zero pickup lines, and couldn't dance—all of which added to my feelings of inadequacy that hadn't left me since I began feeling this way in my early childhood. I simply wasn't the suave kind of guy who easily approached a girl, and girls were by no means chasing me.

Jerry Georges.

Not like my best friend Jerry Georges, who had one great resume. Besides being a strikingly handsome Latino, he was the class president and varsity star baseball player. Like other young men I began to gravitate toward, like Scott Mitchell, Jerry was macho and smart.

Determined to help land me a girlfriend, Jerry found a girl who was willing to go out with me. That weekend, we double-dated and ended up parking in a local "Lovers' Lane" that overlooked the beach.

Twenty minutes later, Jerry and his date were in the back seat breathing heavily and steaming up the windows while I sat in front with my date, twiddling my thumbs and awkwardly making small talk. I must have died a thousand deaths that night, and was overjoyed when I dropped off my utterly bewildered and disappointed date at her house.

My ugly car.

Throughout my school years, beginning in grade school, I fell at the low end of the age group cutoff. As a result, I was always nearly a year younger than my classmates. For example, I was 17 years of age in my senior year of high school, while the majority of my friends were 18 years old. In teenage years, that's big. My being nearly a year younger than my peers was a major contributor to my shyness and feelings of inadequacy. This substantial age difference put me way behind the social curve.

Shortly after turning 18 and barely graduating high school, I decided to move out of my mother's house so that I could be with my buddies. I was still working at the gas stations and was making enough money to chip in my share of the rent on a local two-bedroom apartment. The Ford that my father had given me had broken down, and my mom got me an ugly, pale blue Plymouth Valiant.

Above, Sue around the time I met her. Right, on one of our typical dates.

Cruising State Street on weekends used to be the big thing for car guys. After work one Saturday night, I got in my car and planned to cruise solo when I spotted a pretty girl driving alongside. Because she looked at me for a few seconds longer than any girl had ever done, I pulled to the curb and we began talking. She introduced herself as Sue Jones, who was a year younger and in her senior year at San Marcos High School. The good news was she was beautiful, which caused me to wonder how I'd managed to attract the attention of such a hottie.

That weekend, we went out on our first date. There was a mutual chemistry. She seemed as awkward with guys as I was with girls—and we were both virgins, which in the mid-1960s wasn't a rarity. After a few days of talking on the phone and my driving her home from school, we officially became boyfriend and girlfriend.

The following weekend, I had my first encounter with alcohol (besides the bottle of champagne that I drank after my father's wake). I was living at the apartment with Jerry Georges and another room-mate, and we decided to throw a party. Sue and Jerry's date were the first to arrive around 7 o'clock that evening. Because our friends were scheduled to start arriving shortly, Jerry and I decided to indulge in a pre-party drink, just to loosen things up.

Days earlier, Jerry brought home a fifth of vodka and a quart of orange juice, which we learned were the ingredients of a screwdriver. With absolutely no clue as to what the standard proportions were, Jerry took an eight-ounce glass and nearly filled it to the top with vodka, then asked me how much orange juice he should add. Neither one of us had any idea, so Jerry added a splash of orange juice, "mainly for color."

After we displayed the customary macho bravado in front of our dates, we downed that screwdriver (pile driver would be a better description) between us "like men." Twenty minutes later, our first guests arrived. I opened the door and said, "Hi" and then proceeded to pass out, pitching forward, locked kneed, like a bad vaudeville prat-fall and landing squarely on my forehead. Five minutes later, I came to lying on a bed and looked up at Sue, who was kneeling at my side. "What happened?" I said with a slurred voice, a dazed look on my face, and a golf ball sized knot on my head. It's no wonder that since that evening, I've had a strong aversion to alcohol.

Following that dreadful party, I lasted another week at the apart-ment, and then returned to my mom's house. I simply didn't have the wherewithal for living away from home. I didn't know how to do my laundry or cook or market—nothing. After moving back in with my mom, she convinced—no, ordered—me to enroll at Santa Barbara City College.

That unsightly Plymouth Valiant was equally short-lived. Because I was still working and earning a paycheck, I convinced my mother to help me purchase a used white 1963 Galaxy Ford.

That was one set of hot wheels. Powered by a 427 cu. in. engine and dual carbs, in 1963 the Ford Galaxies dominated NASCAR. Tiny Lund won the first and biggest race of the year, the Daytona 500, with 427s finishing first through fifth.

I took that car, which I named the "White Tornado," out that night and blew the engine street racing. Because my mother didn't have the money to help me get the car repaired at the Ford dealership, I brought the car to Fred's garage with my buddy Mike Dockery. Over several weeks, we took the engine apart, meticulously blueprinting every nut and bolt as we went along.

After putting the engine back together, we were astonished to find that we had a coffee can full of nuts and bolts that somehow didn't find their way back into the engine. Even worse, Mike was fairly certain that he had inadvertently dropped a bolt into the engine's dual carburetors, which meant that it was somewhere inside one of the engine's four-inch cylinders.

After mulling over the problem for what seemed an eternity, Mike pointed with finality at the driver's seat. "Go ahead and fire her up."

"What?!" I replied, aghast. "That could blow the engine! And maybe worse!"

"So what's the alternative? We could take the engine apart again and add more nuts and bolts that coffee can when we put it back together, or take our chances starting it."

In a command, spur of the moment decision, I muttered an obscenity under my breath "This is a dumbass move, Rick" and then slipped in behind the wheel. After saying a silent prayer, I turned the ignition. To our utter bewilderment, the engine instantly started and then roared to life, purring like a kitten. As to the bolt that Mike had dropped into one of the car's cylinders, the engine unbelievably miraculously spit it out the car's exhaust. Hallelujah! Amen, brothers and sisters!

Now that I was back in action, I began taking the indestructible "White Tornado" to the drag races. Because I couldn't afford slicks, the tires would burn rubber through the entire quarter mile. Even though I didn't have the bucks to buy traction bars and other necessary equipment to make my car competitive, I kept attending the drag races, anyway.

The White Tornado; a 1963 Ford Galaxy.

It wasn't long before the stress on the transmission became too much, and I began blowing out rear ends. My brother and I got so good at installing a new rear end that we could do it in 15 minutes. We were right up there with an amateur pit stop team. It got to the point where I'd blow a rear end and I'd say, "Okay, let's jack it up. We know how this works."

In the mid-1960s, unmarried couples didn't dare live together because society simply didn't allow it. So after dating for a year, Sue and I married. I was 19 years old and she was 18. Our families were both highly supportive of our union. After a big wedding and honeymoon, we settled into our first apartment on Red Rose Way and decorated it with sparse furnishing. We didn't have much, except the joy of finally being together as husband and wife.

The Christmas three years after the death of my dad, and after I'd finished unwrapping my "little and medium-sized" gifts, my mother told me to go outside to see my "big toy." It took me all of five seconds to race out the front door to discover a brand new midnight blue 1966 Mustang fastback with a huge red ribbon and bow tied around it. Back then, that highly-prized car among teenagers cost around $3,000. Without a doubt, and on many levels, my mom was the coolest mom in the world.

My first year married to Sue was wonderful. I continued attending Santa Barbara City College and working part-time at the gas stations. As was the case in high school, I didn't socialize in school and hang out with any of the other students. When classes let out, I went to work, and when my shift ended, I drove home. Sue and I were comfortable living a simple existence.

Life was not so peaceful outside the confines of our tiny one-bedroom apartment. Across America, its citizens were divided over the escalating war in Vietnam where American soldiers, many just out of high school, were dying by the hundreds. The nightly news was filled with film footage of bloody massacres, napalm bombings, ambushes, and the body bags of the dead being flown back to the US on military transport planes.

Muhammad Ali (then Cassius Clay) refused to go to war, famously stating that he had "no quarrel with the Viet Cong" and that "No Viet Cong ever called me nigger." Speaking at Riverside Church in New York, Martin Luther King Jr. stated that "somehow this madness must cease. I speak for the poor of America who are paying the double price of smashed hopes at home and death and corruption in Vietnam." Weeks later, more than a thousand police attacked 10,000 peace marchers at the Century Plaza Hotel in Los Angeles, where President Lyndon B. Johnson was being honored. When I fell off to sleep each night, I feared I might be awakened by the sound of war drums.

I didn't like college academia any more than I liked high school academia. I watched the clock and counted off the minutes until I could get in my car and see Santa Barbara City College disappearing in my rearview mirror. To no one's surprise, I eventually got kicked out of City College for having a D minus grade point average. The school basically sent me a generic letter that said get out of here and don't come back.

In line with the old adage "out of the frying pan and into the fire," not long after getting the boot from school, I was drafted into the Army. The draft letter I received began with "Greetings." Greetings, my ass!

The night before I shipped out, Sue and I gathered at my mother's house with both of our families. It was truly a sad time. As hard as I tried, I couldn't hide the stark reality that I was terrified. There was no question that I was ill-equipped to enter the military. In many ways, I was still wet behind the ears.

Sue and I arranged to close down the apartment after I left, and she was to return to live with her parents. My mom saw my being drafted for what it was—her immature, ill-prepared son was in all likelihood headed for the jungles of Vietnam where the war was heating up.

Chapter 4:

Men Will Make Men

U pon being drafted into the Army, I traveled in the predawn hours to Los Angeles where I officially reported for duty. On the first day of indoctrination, after being given a range of tests, I was escorted onto a DC-3 aircraft and flown to El Paso, Texas to start my basic training at Fort Bliss.

During the flight to El Paso, I couldn't stop thinking about Jerry. Shortly after graduating from high school, Jerry enlisted in the Marines and was sent off to Vietnam to fight for his country. He was three weeks from completing his two-year tour of duty when he was killed by a shoulder launched missile. I'd done my best to block the memory of his death from my mind, but now it had returned, and I was left wondering if I was headed to the same hellhole where Jerry lost his life. He was yet another man in my life who was gone, and now I was headed to a place where men make men.

I landed in El Paso at three in the morning, totally petrified. Immediately after the bus door slammed open, a gargantuan drill instructor with his thick web belt slung around his neck stormed onto the bus and began yelling and screaming. Grabbing his new "girls" by their collars and jackets, he unceremoniously kicked everyone off the bus and into the near-freezing early morning chill.

This horrifying introduction to basic training didn't let up for several months. It was the military's job to scare the living daylights out of me so that they could turn me into a killing machine. In order to help with my new identity, they shaved my head and drilled into my brain that I was part of their war effort. Like tens of thousands of America's youth drafted into the military, I soon learned to answer stock questions by root.

"What's the spirit of a bayonet?" my drill instructor barked.

"To kill—Sir!"

"What does the bayonet love?"

"Blood—Sir!"

The first night, I was exposed to live fire in training. I was to walk down a ditch and then low-crawl over a telephone pole while machine guns fired live rounds three feet over my head. I knew I was going to die. Tracers (every fifth round) could be seen, and there were fake mortars exploding all around me.

The night before, one of the soldiers who was crawling under the barb wire ran into a Texas rattlesnake. Instinctively, he jumped up and was instantly killed by one of the machine guns. We'd been warned to "let the rattlesnakes bite you," but this soldier paid the ultimate price for reacting to his gut instead of his brain. I kept crawling under the wire, making myself small, sweating, shaking until I got near the machine gun nest and threw a dummy grenade to show I had completed the live fire course.

In many ways, I was still a momma's boy. I simply wasn't prepared for any of this. One of many examples was the day I was exposed to tear gas, which is a chemical weapon that causes severe eye, respiratory, and skin irritation, pain, vomiting, and even blindness.

Wearing a gas mask, I crawled through mud and under barb wire. Then I walked into a gas room where I was ordered to take off the mask and breathe in the gas. I immediately teared up uncontrollably and it was nearly impossible to breathe. I was so disoriented that when a lieutenant asked me if I was from San Marcos, my high school alma mater, I replied while choking and frothing from my mouth, "No, I'm from New York!"

Moreover, the way the Army treated me made a huge contribution to my feelings of inadequacy. Within days of being subjected to basic training and hearing sound bites of the war atrocities, I laid in my bunk every night and whispered the Lord's Prayer because I was afraid I'd be killed in Vietnam. After all, if Jerry Georges with all his skills couldn't survive, I wouldn't stand a chance.

Being in the Army was the first time I was forced to do something against my will. Worst of all, I'd been jerked away from my new bride when we were just starting a life together, and now she was left alone at home, worried sick that she could become a widow.

Eventually, basic training destroyed whatever identity and connection I had to the life I'd left in Santa Barbara. I no longer had a clue as to where I was going or when I'd return, if I'd return at all.

Although I understood that drill instructors had a job to do, the reality was that they were the worst order of control freaks. It seemed that I was always standing in line, and no matter what line I stood in, I was yelled at. I became disgusted when I'd witness an overweight kid standing in the chow line—a kid who clearly had led a sheltered life—and a drill instructor walks up to this young man and screams in his ear, "You keep your baby paws off that bread, you fat piece of shit!"

Before being drafted into the Army, I rarely experienced people who abused authority. The Army so far presented me with a massive, daily dose of this. Instinctively I didn't like it and had to do all I could to keep the aggression I was feeling in check. Until I saw my dad's friend break the neck of that jack rabbit, I didn't have that compassion. And now I was having it in spades.

A month into basic training, I was sitting with a group of recruits and one of them said to me, "Hey, Rick, do you realize how much you're saying 'fuck'?" His observation got my attention because the truth was that throughout my childhood and teenage years, I wasn't allowed to curse in our house, and if I did, I got slapped or had my mouth washed out with soap. And now every other word was fuck,

Basic training.

and I realized that this was because I was miserable—and angry—and I didn't like what I was becoming.

Upon completing my basic training in Fort Bliss, I received orders that I was being shipped to Fort Ord, which was located in Northern California on the beautiful Monterey Bay Peninsula. Because I'd scored well with numbers, the Army assigned me to radio teletype and Morse code school.

For days, I was stuck in a tiny cubicle for eight hours tapping out Morse code. After a week, many of the other recruits in nearby cubicles couldn't take it any longer and began bitching and complaining.

To them, a few days doing KP and cleaning latrines would be a welcome respite over this brain-squashing monotony. During this time, two recruits had nervous breakdowns from hearing dots and dashes in their ears for eight hours a day. In sharp contrast, because of the many months I was a ham operator during my childhood in East Bronx, I was drawn to this type of schooling and came to believe that I was born for it.

When I had leave, I'd hitchhike from Ford Ord to Santa Barbara. The first time my mom saw me in uniform, she gave me a wonderful look. By then, I was becoming proud to wear the uniform and couldn't wait to show it off to my family.

From when I was a young child playing under the dinner table, I had Friday night dinners with my grandparents. It was a tradition. The first time I arrived home on leave, my grandfather and I got into a discussion about the Vietnam War. Understandably, I'd become indoctrinated into the Army's pro-war position, and my grandfather and the rest of my family sided with the growing number of Americans who vehemently opposed the war. I couldn't understand why my grandfather was taking this anti-war position. The more I tried to defend our military's presence in Vietnam, the more he argued against it. Days later, on my way back to Fort Ord, I wondered what other areas of my thinking the Army had heavily influenced.

Upon completing my Morse code training at Fort Ord, I was sent to Fort Gordon, Georgia. It was autumn when I arrived in Augusta, and the weather was cold, especially at night. Soldiers who pulled fire watch spent an eight-hour shift shoveling coal into furnaces that kept the barracks warm.

During one week, we lived in freezing tents that were only marginally kept warm by kerosene heaters and used our steel helmets to shave and shower. The military was unpredictable this way. I never knew what living conditions awaited me at any point down the road. The Army could ship me anywhere at the drop of a helmet.

The longest time I'd been away from Sue was eight weeks into basic training. Because neither of us could stand the separation any longer, she traveled to Augusta, Georgia in the Mustang with her mother and paid for two rooms at a local motel. The night they arrived, I slipped on my fatigues and snuck off base. After I found my way to the motel, Sue and I enjoyed a long anticipated reunion. In the predawn hours, I snuck back onto the base. To this day, I can't believe I did that. It just wasn't like me.

The reason the Army sent me to Fort Gordon was to learn how to listen to Morse code, and then send it through a teletype machine that would punch holes in a tape that the military would send out through a crypto box. When the response message came back reverse-coded, I'd put it into the machine that would read it out.

This highly-advanced process was called crypto technology that would be reprogrammed every 24 hours by changing the box's wiring. Cryptography prior to the modern age was effectively synonymous with encryption, which is the conversion of information from a readable state to apparent nonsense. I was the top soldier of 33,000 GIs who went through that school, and it turned out that when it came to this communications conversion process, I was a genius at it.

Upon graduating from Fort Gordon, I received orders to travel to a place that none of my fellow soldiers could pronounce. None of us had any idea where this place was located, although some of the men in my barracks were sure it had to be somewhere in Vietnam. One of the guys suggested that I call the post locator. After getting her on the phone, she told me in a southern drawl, "You're being shipped out to Vicenza."

"Oh, so that's how you say it." I said. "So where is that?"

"I've never heard of it," she replied.

"Is it in Vietnam?" I asked, trying to mask my concern. "Anywhere near Da Nang?"

"Hold on a minute. Let me find out."

That minute was the longest 60 seconds in the history of the universe. When I finally heard the woman return to her phone, I took a deep breath and braced for the worst.

"Hello, you still there?"

"I'm here," I replied in a high voice, as my butt puckered.

"Vicenza is in northeastern Italy," she said.

Italy?! If I had to be drafted into the Army at any time in history, there was no better place in the world that a GI could get sent than Vicenza, Italy. Located 120 miles west of Venice, Vicenza was then and still is a thriving cosmopolitan city with a rich history and culture. Everywhere there are museums, art galleries, piazzas, villas, churches, and elegant Renaissance palazzi.

The first time I saw the puny Italian Fiats, I said to another GI, "God, they have tiny cars here. They look like pregnant roller skates. My White Tornado would eat them for breakfast."

Because of my unworldly youth, I was egotistical and condescending. In some ways, I was a shining example of the "ugly American." I saw the fresco paint on the buildings and thought it made the neighborhood look tacky. To make matters more uncomfortable, I didn't speak Italian.

I became a model soldier, and months after I arrived in Vicenza, I was promoted to sergeant, which allowed me to live off post. Sue joined me. In record time, my overall mood began to improve. I even began to speak the language. I was a noncommissioned officer, and for the first time in my life since being president of the CCC team learned to lead men.

We leased a cozy two-room apartment that was funky by American standards. The first room, which was the living and kitchen area, had a kerosene heater, for which we were given a certain amount of kerosene each month. At night, we'd lock this room and walk across the hall to our second room, which essentially was our bedroom and bathroom. There were no screens in the windows. As weird of a setup

Note the missiles in the background.

as it was, it was charming and romantic. How could it not be, given where we were? Needless to say, Sue and I got along wonderfully. What a fantastic second honeymoon this was, and I had the U.S. Army to thank for it.

In addition to our leased apartment, we bought a '63 Volkswagen. When I had leave, we traveled to London, France, Switzerland, and Spain. Sue adapted well to being an Army wife. I only made around $190 per month, but the Army paid for our housing and food and most everything else.

My military job in Europe was primarily to occasionally take part in war games along the Yugoslavian border. My team was part of a missiles communications/support command. We conducted exercises along the border because Yugoslavia was an East Bloc country.

I had a crew and a sophisticated van that was filled with state of the art technology. Even lieutenants who were in charge of my company weren't allowed inside my van unless they had a secret security clearance. Besides special automatic weapons, we had an incendiary device that would instantly blow up the truck in the event of an enemy raid.

Having finally gotten with the program, I made the Honor Guard that often required me to wear dress blues. My khaki uniforms were tailored, and I had spit and polish boots and placed cardboard in my blouse trousers to make them look sharp. My Army uniform and experience gave me the sense that I finally belonged to something mature and masculine. While it didn't feel like a total rite of passage, it felt as if I was finally on that road.

I earned the Soldier of the Quarter honors that represents the Army motto "This We'll Defend," which refers to our nation. This allowed me to also become a member of the NATO Honor Guard. Given that Italy belonged to NATO, I would suit up to meet visiting VIPs and political dignitaries.

As part of my Soldier of the Quarter honors, I was rewarded a

Honor Guard.

military parade and a weekend vacation trip to West Berlin. Due to my secret crypto clearance, the military shipped me through East Germany on an armed train. I felt a bit guilty over receiving these honors, given there were other soldiers receiving Purple Hearts for distinguishing themselves on the battlefields, and all had been wounded in battle. And here I was the Soldier of the Quarter because I'd become a model soldier living a comfortable life in Vicenza, Italy.

At one point in my sojourn to West Berlin, I was awakened by the clatter of the train wheels and a sudden burst of the train's whistle. I looked out the window, and in the moonlight saw the Brenner Pass, which is a mountain pass through the Alps along the border between Italy and Austria. Since that moment, I've never seen anything so beautiful. I could only look at the moonlit sky and say thank you.

On the way to Berlin, the train pulled into the station at East Germany, I spotted a young Soviet soldier standing guard beside a pole. He was wearing his big Soviet Army hat and was bundled up in a mammoth overcoat. It was clear that he was freezing and that the cold had undermined his confidence level, especially given that I was looking back at him from my warm sleeper.

When he spotted me looking at him through the train's window, he glanced away and then came around to the other side of the pole and gave me a friendly smile and brief salute. I remember at the time thinking that here I was at opposite sides of the Cold War with this young Soviet soldier, and yet he wanted me to know that it wasn't personal. He must have felt as I did that it has always been the nature of man to have a few heads of government declare wars on countries in an attempt to take over those countries, and they do so on the backs of the young people, and yet we allow it to happen. It was with honest sincerity that I smiled back at the young soldier and returned his brief salute.

The military changes a person for the good or for the bad. There's nothing in between. The Army was an honorable place to be, but the honor is in the guys who came before me and since.

Army basketball team. I'm on the bottom row, far right.

Nowhere was this feeling more prevalent than each day at sunset when the flag was lowered and the Army had its Call to the Colors. Regardless of where I was on base, I heard a bugle play a sad and moving melody over a loudspeaker. It was like pointing to a religious place. I'd turn to the flag and salute while it was being lowered. Every evening, I did that and said a silent thank you to the tens of thousands of vets who had given their lives. That was what I was told to do — to think about this. The wonderful part of being in the armed services are the traditions and the honor that goes with them.

Six weeks before I was to be discharged from the military, I quite by accident stumbled upon Sergeant Dixon, who was practicing these strange physical movements in back of the barracks. When I inquired as to what he was doing, he told me that he was practicing the martial arts, specifically Tae Kwon Do, whatever that was.

In the late 1960s, the martial arts were practically unknown in the United States. Prior to my seeing Dixon doing these moves, I'd watched and was intrigued by the movie *In Like Flint* starring James Coburn, who performed some primitive basic karate moves that today would be laughable.

Because of my persistence in wanting to learn the rudimentary karate moves that Dixon was practicing, he agreed to teach me a half dozen basic punches, blocks, kicks, and a stance. Back then, I had no idea how good he was, but what he accomplished was that he instilled in me an interest in the martial arts.

Upon completing my two-year tour of duty, I was honorably discharged from the Army. In the end, I felt it was a great tour. I made rank, matured, learned discipline, and even played on our company's basketball and football teams. In many ways, the Army turned out to be good for me, mainly because it helped me gain a degree of focus. Before I was drafted, I was flunking out of school and had an ill-defined future, at best, so maybe the military was what I needed.

Chapter 5:

Bushido, the Warrior's Code

Two years had passed, and the society I returned to was far different. The new hippie culture was in full swing, along with its psychedelic music, drugs, tie-dye shirts, love beads, sit-ins, love-ins, People's Park, and Woodstock. Protesters were everywhere, especially on the college campuses, protesting everything from the Vietnam War to red meat.

Regarding this radical movement, an issue of *TIME* magazine summed it up well in its cover story, "The Hippies: The Philosophy of a Subculture." The article described the guidelines of the hippie code: "Do your own thing, wherever you have to do it and whenever you want. Drop out. Leave society as you have known it. Leave it utterly. Blow the mind of every straight person you can reach. Turn them on, if not to drugs, then to beauty, love, honesty, fun." None of this was for me.

Realizing there was no future in returning to the gas station, I found a job working nights at the phone company where I repaired switches and wiring. It was the only job that translated from being a radio teletype crypto operator in the Army. My high school buddy Scott Mitchell was working there, as well.

Two months after Sue and I returned from Italy, we learned that she was pregnant. Then on January 7, 1970, she gave birth to a healthy baby girl whom we named Dianne. In addition to being a husband, I was now a proud father. Both Sue's family and my family were overjoyed with our new addition. Sue and I were beginning to live the American Dream. Our home became the epitome of mom and apple pie. Santa Barbara's version of the Cleaver Family was well on its way.

I enrolled in Santa Barbara City College. Two years earlier when I was shown the door, my grade point average was a D minus. My first year after reenrolling, I made the Dean's Honor List, which pleased my mother to no end. As I'd done previously, I had no social life at City College. When classes ended, I either went home or to work.

I did, however, have one extracurricular activity. While attending City College, I decided to continue learning the martial arts. My motivation was simply that I didn't feel that I could defend myself if confronted with physical violence. Although I'd been lifting weights for a couple of years, lettered in wrestling in high school, and the military helped put muscle on me, I was still small in stature, 20 lb. heavier at 142.

Having done considerable research on the martial arts, I found a small Kenpo Karate school located on State Street. One afternoon I drove to the school and cautiously entered. As I was soon to discover, back in the late 1960s, it was amazing what power the lay public bestowed upon men who knew karate, especially those who wore a black belt. Mysterious, intimidating, at times even cryptic, many of these men were revered as superhumans, if not gods.

I stood in the entryway and looked around. The small school was approximately 800 square feet. Everything was partitioned off and painted black. It was quiet, almost too quiet. Moments later, the

Paul Wagner.

school's owner and head instructor, Paul Wagner, exited from his office and introduced himself. He was wearing a martial arts uniform, and I instantly noticed the frayed black belt tied around his waist.

Over the next 20 minutes, Paul gave me a brief description and physical demonstration of Kenpo Karate. He was a quiet man with striking eyes and a general aura of kindness. But when he moved, his body exploded with devastating power and speed. In an uncanny sense, he was the embodiment of the hard/soft ying-yang.

The American Kenpo that Paul Wagner taught had its origins in Chinese circular motion with many of its beautiful, graceful movements having come from observing animals, for example the tiger, crane, monkey, snake, and praying mantis. I could never dance or do anything with any degree of grace, but I felt that I could do what Paul had shown me and became determined to learn this exotic art form. Everything about the Asian aspect of the martial arts attracted me, particularly its Bushido (Warrior's Code) and the high value martial

Left, me in tournament competition, and below, Fighting John Natividad.

artists placed on honor and respect. Over time, Paul became another man in my life to show me the way.

I'd been sparring for six months when I started competing in karate tournaments shortly after I earned my blue belt. On weekends, I drove to Los Angeles where most of the tournaments were held. Because I lived in Santa Barbara, I was an outsider to LA's mainstream martial arts community where many of the black belts knew one another and regularly competed together. It was only point sparring, which meant there was no contact to the head, although moderate body contact was allowed.

The next step was to advance to green belt. While testing, I tore a section of cartilage in my right knee. The pain was excruciating, and my right leg was sufficiently compromised. I should have asked to stop the test and gone immediately to the local emergency room, but an inner voice commanded me to continue. Was it the voice of my wrestling coach Mangus? There would not be any more quitting in my life, injury or not. Forever I would abide by this self-imposed rule. This was the first time in my adult life that I was willing to "sell out for what I was trying to accomplish—to be all in." Determined to achieve my goal, I tightly wrapped my knee in duct tape and finished—and passed—the test. Coach Mangus, thank you for teaching me about no quit.

After I graduated from City College with an A.A. degree in 1970, I applied to Cal Poly in San Luis Obispo. The day I received the letter from Cal Poly was a momentous day. Because of my early history of failing out of school and doing poorly on tests, the letter sat on my table for most of the day because I was afraid to open it.

Gaining acceptance to Cal Poly wasn't a shoe in. Unlike the University of California's colleges, students applying for admission to Cal Poly weren't automatically accepted if they had a high enough GPA or number of transferring units. Acceptance to Cal Poly was solely up to the discretion of the college's admissions office.

By nightfall, I had summoned up the courage to open the letter and was overjoyed when I read that I'd been accepted. Finally, I could see my life moving forward. My mom was the only person more excited than I was.

Sue, Dianne and I moved to a one-bedroom duplex in Grover City that was two blocks from the train tracks because we were still living on a shoestring budget. The apartment wasn't anything fancy—small rooms, white semi-gloss paint throughout, vinyl floors and a wall heater. But it was clean. Our daughter slept in her crib in our bedroom.

Sue and I were happy in our little sugar shack. It was temporary while I got through school, and we were still close enough to our families. As my mother had done all her life, she continued to live for her children—and now her first grandchild.

After I attained my brown belt, I got permission from Paul Wagner to teach a few students. The duplex came with a single-car garage, which I turned into a small dojo, paneling the walls and carpeting the concrete floor. The few students that I taught helped supplement the income I was making working in a local pet store stacking shelves and cleaning cages and aquariums. Thankfully, I qualified for the GI bill, which helped with my education.

During the week, I continued attending classes at Cal Poly, and twice a week trained at Paul's karate school. Whenever possible, on weekends I traveled to Los Angeles to continue my tournament competition. I had an extremely busy schedule and more than enough on my plate. I felt driven like never before—toward what, at this early stage, I had no idea. I would remain driven to this day.

Eventually, I became friends with a group of fellow competitors, including Chuck Norris, Mike Stone, Steve Fisher, Cecil Peoples, Gene LeBell, John Natividad, Ted Tabura, Ted Wong and his troupe, Eric Lee, and James Lew. Along with others, we'd party on Friday and Saturday nights and then spar each other the following day.

I'd often place first in my division, but I'd never win the grand championship. Then one weekend I won the grand championship at Ron Chapel's tournament, which was a proud day for me, especially when I reflected back to the days when I was a wimpy kid in the Bronx. A year later, I won a trophy at the biggest tournament in the United States—the coveted Long Beach Internationals that was founded by Kenpo Grandmaster Ed Parker.

After diligently practicing karate for a couple of years, Sue became a competent martial artist in her own right and was awarded the rank of brown belt. Although she didn't have an interest in competing in tournament sparring, she was drawn to competing in kung-fu forms and weapons. Besides studying with me, she was taught by the legendary Eric Lee, who from 1970 – 1974 was heralded as "The King of Kata," having amassed over 100 world titles in kata competition.

Eric Lee was friends with Kim Kahana, who was one indestructible Hawaiian. Kim served as a paratrooper in the Korean War where

Sue competing in weapons.

Kim Kahana.

he was captured and shot by an enemy firing squad. Feigning death, he was left by his captors in a mass grave from which he escaped after the North Koreans left. Then in 1955, he survived a plane crash in the state of Texas that killed the 32 other people on board. Kim's martial arts performing career began as a knife and fire dancer in a stage show called *Samoan Warriors*.

Sue and I got invited to Kim's house that was located in Chatsworth. After I'd been there a while, I noticed over his fireplace mantel pictures of Kim with many of Hollywood's legendary actors—John "Duke" Wayne, Telly Savalas, Jimmy Stewart, Paul Newman, Charles Bronson, Sylvester Stallone, and Tom Sellick.

When I asked Kim about the photos, he told me that he'd worked with many of the actors as a Hollywood stuntman. For the better part of the afternoon, we talked about stunt work, which I found highly intriguing.

Kim's home was situated on a big piece of property in Chatsworth in the San Fernando Valley where in later years, under the banner of the Kahana Stunt School, he taught students how to do high falls and fights. When Kim asked me if I was interested in doing stunt work in Hollywood, I replied, "When do we start?"

There was a Catch 22, however, which was that in order to work on a Hollywood film production, I had to become a member of the Screen Actors Guild (SAG), which wasn't easy. Kim promised to help me with the process. In the meantime, I arranged to drive to his home on weekends to begin learning the basics of stunt work.

As I began my second year at Cal Poly, I started to become disenchanted. Once again, I found myself taking a battery of vocational tests that were followed by a face-to-face meeting with one of the college's guidance counselors.

"Well, Rick, what do you think you'd like to major in?" the woman began.

"I have no idea," I replied.

"Well, what do you like to do?"

"You mean besides surfing, drag racing, and the martial arts?"

"We don't have those majors here."

"Of course," I offered with a weak smile.

"It appears you like sports."

"I like wrestling,"

"Do you like to read?"

"Sure," I replied, not wanting to disagree with the woman.

"Great. Why not major in English with a minor in physical education?"

Really? Again? She went on to explain that this would require my taking courses in kinesiology, anatomy, statistics, and journalism. What an odd mix. I wondered where all that would lead after I graduated. Was I to become a massage therapist who recited poetry to my clients? There had to be a better way, and it turned out there was.

In 1972 when I was in my last semester at Santa Barbara City

College, Paul Wagner offered to sell me his karate school for a thousand dollars. He wanted to enjoy life without the stress of running a martial arts school. He moved to Ventura where he opened a health food store (sorrowfully, Paul passed away in April 2016). Although his proposition sounded interesting, I knew nothing about running a karate school. Paul told me that I could attend Tracy's business school in New Jersey and, upon graduating, buy a franchise.

It all sounded good to me. I told Sue that I wanted to quit college and buy Paul's school, and she was in favor of it. When I told my mother about my decision—Look out! Oh boy!—it practically broke her heart. And my neck!

"You're giving up college to teach karate?" she asked disbelievingly.

"I'm buying a business, Mom. I'm doing more than teach karate." Reluctantly, she finally consented and said she would hope for the best.

Sue had an equally busy workload. Besides being the consummate homemaker who superbly ran the household and took great care of our beautiful daughter who was joy personified, she began working at the country courthouse, first as a clerk, and later as a deputy marshal. Additionally, having developed her own interest in the martial arts, she began studying under me. After a few months, we concluded that if we were going to spend time together on weekends, she needed to start traveling with me to Los Angeles.

We moved with the baby to a rented house in Goleta, and a few weeks later, I traveled to New Jersey and arrived at the Tracy Brothers Business School that was run by Kenpo black belts Al and Jim Tracy. When I arrived for my first day of instruction, which was being held at a house, I expected to be taught by two Herculean athletes.

Al Tracy wasn't there when I arrived. I waited in the downstairs living room and finally saw a pair of skinny, knobby legs in a bathrobe coming down the staircase. It was Jim Tracy. This was the start of the business course that initially looked to be a huge disappointment. Things, however, didn't turn out that way. Al and Jim Tracy were excellent businessmen whose business formula had a history of remarkable success.

The Tracy brothers taught the Arthur Murray Dance sales method of business. After I returned to Santa Barbara and closed the deal on purchasing the school, I made $4,000 my first week. I charged $495 a year and gave each new enrollee the option of making one full payment or paying $195 down and making monthly payments. Every new student got one private lesson per week. The Tracy method resulted in my building up my school enrollment. My karate school was going to be my life. In time, I planned on opening a chain of schools.

A short while after becoming the head instructor and sole owner of Paul's school, I tested three times for my black belt. My initial test was with Paul Wagner, followed by my second test that was conducted by Richard "Dick" Willet and required that I fight six black belts to receive my "staff promotion" in the Tracy system.

My third test was by heavyweight world karate champion Joe Lewis under the banner of his "Joe Lewis Systems." After one hour of performing all of the self- defense techniques and katas (dance like forms that contain all the techniques), I stood sweating on shaky legs before the heavyweight champion, who said, "We're going to have three rounds of fighting. The first round, I'm going to be an evasive fighter"—so basically Joe just wore me out, staying away from me, tapping kicks away. After the first round, he said, "Okay, this next round I'm going to be a blocker and jammer." For the next several minutes he got in tight and blocked everything I threw at him. Then for the final round, he said he was going to be the aggressor. Oh shit.

If a person gave Joe respect, he fought that person hard, but gave them respect in return. He had a huge influence on improving my self-confidence. Because I was small in stature, especially in comparison to heavyweight fighters like Joe Lewis and Mike Stone. I felt that

With Joe Lewis and daughter Dianne.

I had to put forth ten times the effort of a bigger opponent in order to win. Joe told me to stop thinking that way. "Rick, don't look at your opponent and all the muscles he has. Everybody has a nose, a solar plexus, and a groin. And that's all you should see when you fight."

Joe was one of the top three most impressive martial artists I've met. He was a man with an enormous heart who simply didn't have

With Grandmaster Ed Parker.

quit. Like Jerry George and Scott Mitchell, Joe was another role model that I tried to emulate. When in 1983, at age 40, he fought to regain his heavyweight championship title by fighting Kerry Roop, it was a raging bull movie. In the final rounds of what was a slugfest, Joe was bloodied all over. I broke down and cried while watching it. The reality was Joe was too old to be fighting. He got his ass kicked, but he fought like his life depended on it, which was the way he taught. Joe was grit exemplified and a man with no quit.

The day I made black belt challenged my warrior's mindset. When I went through the promotional ceremony and tied my black belt around my waist, I couldn't believe that I was a black belt. Although I knew I'd earned it by passing my test, the belt was so sacred in my mind that I felt I shouldn't be wearing it and was even hesitant about putting it on. I had so much respect for that belt and the people who had come before me that it took a long while before it felt comfortable tied around my waist.

As an aside, although by no means less important, in addition to holding black belt rank under Al and Jim Tracy, as well as rank under Joe Lewis, in July of 1986 I was promoted to the rank of 5th degree black belt by American Kenpo Grandmaster Ed Parker, and in April 2016 promoted to the rank of 7th degree black belt by American Kenpo Grandmaster Mike Pick.

Now that I was a black belt, I became trophy hungry because I felt that displaying a vast array of trophies in my school would be good for business. Within six months of attaining my black belt, my school became so popular in Santa Barbara that I opened a second school—"Karate Center International"—in neighboring Goleta. Additionally, I began instructing at the Santa Barbara Y.M.C.A., did many demos throughout Santa Barbara County, and produced two full contact karate tournaments that brought together the Northern and Southern halves of the state.

The first tournament was a local tournament. Because of its success, ESPN sent a camera crew to film my second tournament that was held at Santa Barbara's Earl Warren Showgrounds. Both tournaments were held around the time the Professional Karate Association (PKA) was initially formed and turned a good profit. One of the highlights for me was coming to the showgrounds and seeing all the people lined up purchasing tickets to this new full contact karate.

Trophy hungry.

The only downside occurred at my second tournament when one of the fighters got knocked out and went into seizures. I stood on the sidelines while the medical staff feverishly worked on him, terrified that he was going to die. It was frightening. I felt guilty as a promoter that I was making money. Although I wasn't charging the fighters to fight (in fact, I was paying them to fight), I was making money from ticket sales. Thank God the fighter survived. Had he died, his memory would have haunted me for the rest of my days.

Being the owner and head instructor of a karate school resulted in my being an open target to challenges. Every few months, some hothead would walk into my school looking to make a name for himself. Mine wasn't the only school in Santa Barbara. In fact, there were several schools, and we were competitive with each other.

One day, I received a phone call from Bill Berk, who was the head of the local Shotokan karate school. "Be careful, Mr. Avery," he said. "A big guy walked into my school yesterday and just stood there staring at me. I threw a couple of hard snap kicks at my students and he walked out." After making a mental note of the man's description, I thanked Bill, who was a large, muscular man, himself, and hung up.

At that time, I was renting out space to a Chinese man named Mr. Lim, who taught tai chi, which is a gentle exercise that can also be used as self-defense. He had just finished teaching a class and was going through one of his forms while I was closing up the studio. The last of Lim's students walked out the back door of the school just as a big guy entered through the front door. The guy fit the description of the person described to me over the phone by Bill Berk—around six feet tall, 200 pounds, muscular and stocky.

Turning his attention to Lim, who was on the mat finishing his graceful tai chi form, the guy engaged Lim in meaningless conversation and then asked, "What would you do if I pushed you?"

The guy's attitude caused my antennae to go up. Lim replied, "Well, I'd circle my arms around and I would push you back with my chi."

"Your what?" the guy asked in a louder voice.

"My chi—my inner energy."

"Really? And you could demonstrate that for me?"

"Certainly," Lim said with a smile.

I thought, *Oh, God, this is going to go bad.*

Suddenly, the guy pushed Lim into one of several floor-to-ceiling wall mirrors, breaking it into several large pieces and causing Lim to fall to the ground.

In that instant, I realized that I either jump in or I don't. There was no in-between. I had been taking lessons from Tadashi Yamashita, who taught me the nunchaku, bo, and the tonfa. He talked about if I ever had to fight somebody in my school, I needed to beat them to

With Tadashi Yamashita.

the point where I would have to lift them into a chair, at which time I would beat them some more, so that they would never come back. With those words flashing in my mind, I jumped in.

When the guy advanced on the fallen tai chi instructor, I threw a punch. At the time, I did demonstrations that included breaking boards and bricks with my fists. I hit this guy in the temple as hard as I could. The punch knocked him down, and then he got up and gave me a look that said, *what was that?*

Visibly frightened, Lim jumped up and ran from the school. The guy stood up and started toward me. I delivered kicks to his groin and knees. I was completely ineffective. I was a black belt and nothing was working! I was learning the grim reality of a street fight as to what works and what doesn't. There would be no neighborhood mother to break this one up.

Before I knew it, the guy had me cornered and grabbed me, forcing me against the back wall as we continued fighting on the tatami mats. The lights were off, and I could barely see anything. I ripped tuffs of hair from his skull and stuck my thumb in his eye, trying to pop it out. Nothing stopped this animal. Was he on PCP, mentally crazed, or just bloody strong?

To my right, on the side wall hung an array of wooden weapons. As I finally managed to duck and break away from him, he grabbed a wooden katana sword from the wall and savagely broke it over my head. I nearly blacked out as blood began oozing from my scalp. I panicked as my options and skills ran out. I grabbed a pair of nunchakus from the wall and swung them, hitting him twice in his knees. He stumbled backwards and fell. I felt a moment of relief, but then, like a rising phoenix, he got up and walked menacingly toward me again.

He was indestructible, and there was no doubt in my mind at this point that I was in a life or death struggle. With my every last bit of strength, I smashed the nunchaku across the side of his head. He dropped! It's over . . . then he slowly got to all fours and started at me again. I thought, *I'm dead.* He fell down again, and then stood up on wobbly legs slowly started a retreat, stumbling out of the school.

I immediately called the police because I was afraid I had killed him. The cops found him in a hospital the next day. My head wound took 18 stitches to close, and the police found a bone chip on the mats that came from the guy's skull, as well as tufts of hair I had pulled out. Oh, yes, he had recently been discharged from a state mental institution.

Since that horrifying encounter, I've had a serious talk with every student I've taught. I tell them that being hit in the face by someone who is intent of doing serious harm is a huge awakener. If a person has never been hit hard, that person cannot tell me — or themselves — how they're going to react. Over the years, I've met many high ranking black belts who have never been in a street fight. They have no idea what they'll do. Maybe they'll fall down and cry or beg the guy to stop hitting them. The fact that they simply don't know is a major problem.

Beginning in 1973, I became a huge fan of the television show *Police Story*, which detailed the personal lives of the men and women of the Los Angeles Police Department. Don Meredith and Tony Lo Bianco were often seen throughout the run of the show (1973 – 1979) as detectives Bert Jameson and Tony Calabrese, respectively.

My close high school friend Scott Mitchell became a Santa Barbara police officer, and one night he invited me to go with him on a ride along. I went to roll call with him and was greeted by a Watch Commander Lt. Strong and Sgt. Rochester, who apparently had a bone to pick with their officers. Sgt. Rochester wanted to know who had superglued his desk drawers closed and his coffee cup to the desk after pissing in it. I couldn't believe what I was hearing. He held up cartoons by Mike Fitzmorris, who was the satirist of the group, chewing him out. It was embarrassing, but I was drawn to this great a dysfunctional group of misfits that I would later discover were extremely good at being cops.

After roll call, Scott was issued his shotgun and we went outside to his patrol car. Right out of the station, he had to respond to a traffic accident. He turned on the siren and overhead lights (Code 3), and off we went. I sat in the front passenger seat, excited that we were speeding through the streets of Santa Barbara. This was better than my high school drag racing days!

When we got to the scene of the accident, I was impressed by how quickly Scott got out of his patrol car and easily took control of a chaotic situation. I watched him confidently walk from the car toward the multiple car injury accident. Crisp uniform, gun on his hip, my pal Scott calmed everyone down, called for an ambulance, cleared the traffic hazards, and even handled the nosey looky-loo bystanders. What he did that night had a tremendous impact on me that changed the course of my life.

Chapter 6:

To Protect and Serve

By the time I arrived home after my ride-along with Scott, I decided I wanted to be a cop. Unfortunately, when I went to apply for a job with the Santa Barbara Police Department, I was told that they had a minimum six-foot height requirement, which I didn't meet. A year later, however, the height requirement was dropped. Ecstatic, I was the first to fill out a job application. I later learned that approximately 400 job applications had been received— and there were only four slots to fill.

I spent weeks studying for the civil service exam and ran the obstacle course every week. I wanted that job more than anything and was determined to put 1,000 percent effort into it. This determination would carry over into every future life endeavor I would ever embark on.

Over the course of a week, I took a written test, oral test, a civil service test, and also underwent a psychological interview. I was worried sick about all the exams because of my history of performing poorly

Above, no more pencil neck here—that's me, second from left. Right, Scott and me.

on tests, as well as a background check that could reveal my poor grades during my first year at City College.

A week later, I gave a huge sigh of relief when I learned that I was one of the four applicants who had been selected and would undergo training at the Ventura County Sheriff's Full Stress Academy. For a couple of years, Scott, a supreme athlete, held the record for the academy's obstacle course. I broke that record because I trained like I was going to compete in an Olympic decathlon.

I later heard through the grapevine that several department officials had their eye on me because they were concerned that I might misuse my martial arts training. Back then, anyone who held a black belt was considered a lethal weapon. At close range, a single karate strike could be as deadly as a bullet. Well, I knew that wasn't always true — just ask that mental patient.

My prior military and martial arts training served me well. When the instructors at the put me through the stress academy in order to see how I would react under pressure, the smile that I offered myself at the end of the course respectfully conveyed, "Is that all they got?" Over time, I became physically and mentally strong. Having increased my weight training, I was 175 pounds of muscle.

Because I graduated the academy and received awards for being the #1 honor cadet and a top marksman, I was hired by the Santa Barbara Police Department. Within six months, I'd reached the status of a mini-celebrity around town because of my popular karate school, my police badge, and my extensive private security work at popular nightspots Salty's Topless Bar, The Feed Store, and Teaser's Restaurant that morphed into a disco dance club at night.

Becoming a cop gave me additional, much needed experience in life. I made good money and was able to buy a house and a new car. Because Sue was also working, we had an excellent joint income. I planned on being a cop for the rest of my life.

I was a fair cop, but I was all business, especially the first year.

Above, enjoying Beat 3. Below, we had a winning team on and off the streets.

I never had an interest in being assigned to a relatively safe beat or having a desk job. Instead, I wanted action and that's why I asked to be assigned to Beat 1 or Beat 3 that were in the worst parts of town on the lower east side.

When I finally landed that assignment, I became determined to clean up Dodge. I started busting people and throwing my weight around, even before backup arrived. I'd walk into 7-11s like I was Wyatt Earp and made my presence known. The dozen or so gang members (many who were armed) could have jumped on top of me beat me senseless, but they chose not to.

I was a badge heavy cop, which is known as the "John Wayne Syndrome"—a self-absorbed, immature cop whose actions and persona are fueled by his monumental ego. I saw only right and wrong. There was no in-between. Cops were supposed to seek out criminals, and then arrest them and haul them off to jail.

After that first year on patrol, word came down from my watch commander that a contract had been put out on me on the lower east side. The department had reliable sources and took it seriously. As a precautionary measure, I was reassigned me to Beat 5 and 6 until the heat cooled down. Although it took a year for me to mellow out, I learned my lesson, which is why a cop, when hired, is on probation for their first year. Eventually, I became more professional and not black and white like my patrol car. Police work has a lot of gray, and I started to see the points of view of both sides.

Many nights when I came home late, I needed to wind down and didn't want to talk about what happened during the day, which made Sue unhappy. Police psychologists say it's important for cops to talk about their job to their spouses, but for me it was about timing. That's where it goes south for many police marriages, and Sue and I had that problem.

This is why most cops only hang out with other cops, which they refer to as choir practice. Choir practice came from the popular novel

With my kids
Dianne and
Brian.

by Joseph Wambaugh entitled *The Choir Boys*. After work, we'd all gather in the parking lot behind the station or a local beach to have a few beers and blow off steam with stories from the past shift. This is called "choir practice." The same is true for combat GIs.

In 1973, Sue and I were blessed with our second child, Brian Edward, who was named after the football player Brian Piccolo (played by James Caan in the movie *Brian's Song)* and Edward after my dad, whom he would never know.

Oftentimes, the best source for me to unwind was with my two children. Dianne and Brian's main focus was on their toys and having Daddy read them a story or play horsey with them or just sit around and be silly. With my children, I was able to resort back to my own carefree childhood days, which was often therapeutic. They gave me unconditional love. Every day, they brought Sue and me tremendous joy.

I never abused the badge or a citizen. I was always fair and knew from my youth the difference between good and evil. I wanted to be the Good Samaritan cop, as hard as that was to do every day.

After two years, I learned to accept what most cops ultimately discover—that cops receive little, if any, positive reinforcement. For example, I would arrest a burglar. I was lucky enough to catch one because burglars were hard to find, let alone catch. But I made the arrest. I had to fight that burglar, so I tore my pants and skinned up my arms and hands. After the fight, I cuffed and transported him to the station where I called Sue and told her I'd be late because I had to file a report. She was not happy.

An hour later, my sergeant took my report and turned it into a road map of red marks that indicated all the places he felt I screwed up. So far, no one told me that I did a great job in catching the burglar. A month later when the case went to court, the judge ruled in the burglar's favor over some technicality and the burglar was set free, often smiling at me in court when the verdict was read or giving me a victory sign a week later when he saw me out on patrol. This was typical. Throughout the six years that I was a cop, I received little positive feedback. Being in law enforcement was a thankless job that eventually soured my outlook on society.

My friend and fellow officer Mike Fitzmorris continued drawing hysterically funny cartoons about the brass and surreptitiously posting them around the station. Many of us warned Mike that he should stop doing that because he could get into more big trouble, but he kept it up and never got discovered. Mike had a photographic memory and in my opinion was the best instinctual, cool headed and dependable cop I ever met.

When I first became an officer, I was proud of it. When someone asked me what I did, I'd tell them. First thing out of their mouth, 90 percent of the time, was "I got a ticket the other day that was really a BS ticket." Then I'd hear about how the person had done nothing wrong, that the cop didn't know the law or needed to fill his ticket quota or didn't like the person's looks or race or gender or God only knows what else. After a couple years of this, I wouldn't tell people I was a cop. Instead, I'd tell them I owned a karate school.

The criminals were far worse. I'd say to a guy six-foot-two that he

CALIFORNIA DEPARTMENT OF JUSTICE
DIVISION OF LAW ENFORCEMENT
INVESTIGATIVE SERVICES BRANCH

ISB CASE NO. ....

ISB use only

New ☐   Additional ☐
Resubmittal ☐

REQUEST FOR A MENTAL
EXAMINATION

REQUESTING AGENCY: ALL PATROLMAN WHO HAVE EVER .... COUNTY OF: ....
worked with the below **raisinbbrain**...   (Location)

OFFENSE: Masturbating with one hand while caressing ball bearing with the other hand.

SUSPECT(S): (Include ID No. if any) ..... SGT. RODCHESTER: aka of Capt. QUIGG, or BALL BEARING

When floundering with KIRKWOOD they assume the role of LENNY and SQUIGY.

VICTIM(S): ...... ANYONE NOT living in the TWILIGHT zone. ....

BRIEF SUMMARY OF CIRCUMSTANCES: .... The purpose of this examination is to

ascertain why cSgt. RODCHESTER suffers from paranoia. Why he continues to believe that anyone would piss in his coffee cup or glue this same cup to his desk with suspected super glue..

EVIDENCE SUBMITTED: (Packages, containers, etc.) # 1. Coffee cup with yellow liquid inside
2. suspected super glue residue . # 3. the body of DeMarco.....

PURPOSE OF EXAMINATION: To ascertain why a Sgt. with many years experience would blow the fuck out of a cigarette thief, and endanger the lives of fellow officers at the same time.- AND TO LET THE ADMINISTRATION KNOW ITS TIME TO TERMINATE THIS WACO.

CHAIN OF CUSTODY			
EVIDENCE RECEIVED FROM	EVIDENCE DELIVERED TO	DATE	TIME

If further information is needed concerning this case, the following official should be contacted:
.... Phone No.: ....

ISB Report to be sent to the attention of: .... FROM THE FILES OF THE OTHER CARTOONIST ....

Evidence should be returned to the attention of: ....

Officer investigating this case: ....

Date results needed by: .... For (type of court and location) ....
....

IS ABOVE LISTED EVIDENCE PROPERLY MARKED AND PACKAGED?
PLACE THIS FORM IN ENVELOPE ON OUTSIDE OF EVIDENCE PACKAGE

ISB-4   29533-552 12-74 100M Ⓓ ⊝ OSP was under arrest, and he'd say "Fuck you, mother fucker." I was raised in the Bronx where cops were rarely disrespected. When someone mouthed off to them in any way, they'd find themselves in a world of hurt.

When I began working on the police force, I was a one person police unit. I didn't have a partner. I'd hook someone up and take that person to jail. If they resisted, I used my martial arts to win the fight and win the day. Not with kicks and punching, but with submissions. If I called for backup, it came fast and furious because most of the cops I worked with wore extra-large uniforms and were old school.

For example, late one night, a young black male was breaking into a house. I surprised him from behind and we ended up getting into a struggle. This guy was a monster and he knew the ropes. Finding myself on the losing end, I cracked my flashlight across the side of his head and put out a code 33, which was a call for immediate help. Within a minute, I heard a stampede of feet, as four burly cops arrived like an F5 tornado and shoved me out of the way—their attitude being, get out of the way, Ricky, we got this—which resulted in my stepping into a pail of used oil and ruining my new shoes.

The following day, the mother of the burglar made a complaint to my lieutenant, claiming that I had cracked one of her son's ribs with my flashlight. The fact that I was fighting for my life didn't appear to concern her. The lieutenant backed me, telling her the facts. She slapped her son on his arm as they left.

In patrol, the first person I saw who died was a mother who was running across Cabrillo Boulevard. It was raining hard that night and everyone's visibility was severely impaired. A driver, who couldn't see through the rain and low lighting, had run over this lady, and to compound the tragedy, her daughter also got hit when she raced into the street to save her.

I arrived code 3, grabbed my first aid kit from my trunk, and ran to the sidewalk where I found that the mother was busted up pretty badly. Bystanders gathered, and a passing nurse rushed to sit down, laying this woman's head in her lap. I lifted her ankle to bandage it, and her foot nearly fell off in my hands. Aghast, I told myself to stay calm, as blood poured all over my hands. The nurse said, "Whatever you're doing, keep doing it because she's breathing better, her pulse is increasing," which is what sometimes happens just before a person dies. She kept bleeding profusely and died moments later, as did her daughter who had tried to save her.

As the ambulance pulled up, I returned to my police car and began putting my first aid gear into the trunk. I stood there for a while, holding my emotions in check. Repressing this type of emotional pain is extremely dangerous for a police officer, or anyone for that matter, because it all piles up and eventually comes back at a later time and place.

But cops don't have the luxury of immediately dealing with emotional pain because they have to get to another call—and one that may well be far worse. Over time, my mind became a cold, dusty, empty place. Whenever I ventured too deeply into its catacombs, I'd get lost, and it became an echo chamber.

I saw gunshot wounds, guys dying right in front of me. Human death rattles became a haunting, albeit familiar, sound. Dead body calls were deplorable. I'd walk into a room where a guy blew his head off with a shotgun and had been dead for several days, lying in his own feces. I couldn't breathe. There is no worse smell than the stench of decaying human flesh being devoured by thousands of maggots. On calls like this, it was common to request the fire department to bring breathing apparatus because no one could breathe the ambient air.

No police officer can ever forget the children. One weekend, I responded to a multiple fatality car accident, again on Cabrillo Blvd., but this time on the east end. As I pulled up, one of my partners was walking toward me, carrying a three-year-old girl in his arms and his lips were red. I kept thinking, *why is he wearing lipstick carrying that baby?* But it wasn't lipstick. It was blood, because he'd been doing mouth to mouth resuscitation on this child, who sorrowfully didn't survive.

When I was a rookie cop, I rolled up on an accident and from a block away thought I could smell brains, which have a unique odor. A drunk had come out of a bar and passed out in the center of the

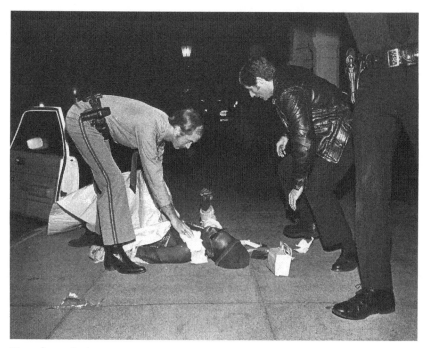

Gunshot victim.

roadway while he lay there unconscious, and a limousine had driven over his head.

When I arrived, the procedure dictated that I immediately call an ambulance, but this guy's skull was broken open and his brains were all over the rear tire and fender. My sergeant arrived and asked if I'd called an ambulance. When I told him I hadn't, he chewed me out. "What are you, a doctor all of a sudden? That's not your job, call an ambulance." I told him to go take a look at this guy and tell me he's not dead. Having to follow the book often put me in the position of being forced to go against common sense that was vital for my own emotional survival. Three people died there. Every time I would pass that place, I would remember. As time passed, those "places" would grow.

Across the boards, the violence that I was subjected to every week turned me around. Being a policeman wasn't the job I thought it was. It wasn't good guys versus bad guys. It wasn't just take the bad guys and put them away. The job turned me into a person I didn't know. I wanted to spend more time with my children, but I sometimes worked all night and saw little of them.

At the police academy, we were told that two things would happen to us if we graduated. First, we had only a 50/50 chance of making it to retirement. I laughed to myself because I was young. Second, if we did make it to retirement, there was a 50 percent chance that we'd become an alcoholic, overweight, divorced—or all three. Again, I scoffed at the entire scenario.

The Santa Barbara Bowl, which has hosted many concerts, is nestled in the foothills north of the city. I was working with my assigned motorcycle partner Officer Derr at a concert given by Willie Nelson. After the concert, we were directing cars out of the canyon when all of a sudden a man on a Vespa scooter almost ran us both over. It seemed intentional. Seriously? He actually thought that two motor cops on REAL motorcycles are going to stand for that?

Almost comically, we hopped on our motorcycles and pursued the motorist in a slow chase, eventually forcing him off the road. He dropped his scooter and tried to run away and started to fight with us, yelling obscenities through a mouth that smelled like a distillery. Over his cursing and flailing, we got him into a sitting position and Officer Derr started to mace him so we could cuff him.

"Derr, stop it, damnit!" I yelled. "You're getting that crap all over me!" I never carried mace because whenever it was used, it made the suspect angrier and often got all over the officer. On a personal level, it reminded me of the tear gas room in the Army. As we finally got the

I'm not Derr.

guy in cuffs, he shouted that he was a doctor and shouldn't be treated this way. Later that night during booking, it was learned that the man was a dentist.

When the case came to trial, he was found guilty of DUI and resisting arrest. This wasn't his first conviction. He had a long record of driving drunk and, because of this and other problems, had lost his license to practice dentistry. Because Officer Derr had signed the arrest report and was the name I yelled out during the arrest, this defrocked dentist had nothing but Derr's name on his mind and was determined to get even.

Days later, we heard in an early morning briefing that the dentist had bought a shotgun and was hunting for Officer Derr. Following the briefing, I went to my motorcycle and drew a big sign that said, "I am not Officer Derr" and put it behind my windshield.

Later that day when a police unit pulled over the dentist near the 101 freeway and Arrellaga Street, he had a pistol grip shotgun on the backseat that he intended on getting even with Officer Derr.

Two years after I joined the Santa Barbara Police Department, my 12-year marriage to Sue ended. Being a policeman had a great deal to do with the failure of my marriage, but there was more to it.

I didn't date much when I was a kid. I married my first girlfriend. Although I truly loved Sue to the best of my ability, when we began dating and married a year later, I didn't have a strong sense of myself. Most importantly, until I entered my late 20s, I rarely had any choices in life. Practically everything about my life was decided by someone else or by circumstances and situations that were devoid of options.

When I was a kid, girls paid no attention to me, and then when I became of age, Sue was the only girl who gave me the time of day. Then ten years later, I was a black belt karate teacher and a buffed cop doing security work in many of Santa Barbara's best pickup night-clubs—and for the first time in my life, women were noticing me.

One afternoon, a 17-year old girl named Joni Schafer walked into my school. She was ungodly beautiful—blonde, sun-streaked hair, radiant emerald green eyes, and a drop-dead gorgeous figure. Most importantly, she paid attention to me, which was something that, until recently, no female except Sue had ever done. I felt utterly powerless under her spell.

That same day, Joni signed up for karate lessons and became my student. Almost immediately, she began looking up to me. She was 17 and I was 28. Although she was young, she had the maturity of someone much older. What initially began as talking together after her lesson soon turned into our having lunch together, then walking together on the beach, and eventually we ended up having an affair.

As much as I cared for Joni, I felt tremendous guilt over the affair and worried constantly that Sue would find out, which ultimately happened. Many of my students at my school knew about the affair, and a few left because they felt that their teacher should have higher standards for himself. Of course, they were right.

Joni.

I knew from the start that what I was doing was wrong. I was raised that marriage vows are for life. More than anything else, I was deeply concerned about our kids because they were so young and had been raised in a two-parent, stable home. But I'd passed the failsafe point and divorce was inevitable.

I've always taken complete responsibility for my failed marriage to Sue. From the day we were married until the day she learned about my affair with Joni, she was the perfect wife in every sense of the word. She lived an honorable life.

After Sue and I divorced, she remained in Santa Barbara for a while, and then moved to Montana with our kids. The separation from my children was emotionally devastating. They were so sweet,

My kids, Dianne, Brian and Me.

innocent, and undeserving of this. For the next ten years, I saw Dianne and Brian only in the summers and holidays. Every time I put them on a plane to fly back to Bozeman, Montana, I bled from my heart guilt, hurt, and self-loathing.

Over the next two years, Joni and I lived together. The reality of having the stigma of the affair behind us, and that we were no longer hiding, allowed our relationship to blossom. The best part was that we were now together all the time, although we still had some adjusting to do because of our substantial age difference. She continued waitressing at Carrows restaurant, while I continued working as a police officer and running my karate school.

On a rainy night in 1976 around Christmas time, I was on patrol when got a call on the radio from Officer Bob Fratilla to meet with the "RP" (reporting party) who was downtown on Ortega Street. The call was in regard to vandalism to a white Jaguar. I drove to the location and looked around, but there was no sign of a white Jag.

When I reported back to Officer Fratilla and told him I couldn't locate the reporting party, he told me to call the station on a telephone, which I found odd. For some reason, he didn't want to continue our conversation over the airwaves.

When I got to a pay phone and called the station, Fratilla said, "Care to guess the name of the person who called in about his car being vandalized?"

"I have no idea, Bob, pray tell," I replied sarcastically.

"It was John Travolta, the actor. And it wasn't a prank call. I recognized his voice."

I was a huge John Travolta fan. His hit movie *Saturday Night Fever* had just come out, and *Welcome Back Kotter* was a top-rated weekly television show. I drove back to State Street, which is the main thoroughfare in Santa Barbara, and stopped at a major intersection. It was pouring rain, and there—almost miraculously—was the white Jaguar stopped beneath an adjacent streetlight. I flashed my overhead lights to get the attention of the driver and waved for him to join me.

As the Jag pulled up and parked in front of me, the rain curiously stopped. I got out of my car and walked toward the Jag just as John Travolta stepped from the driver's side. At the time, he was the most popular actor in the world. A second man stepped from the front passenger side and slowly joined us.

"Hi, guys. Did you call?" I asked. "I understand your car was vandalized?"

Travolta glanced at his car and then looked back at me. "Yes. We've been Christmas shopping, and when we drove away from the mall, a guy jumped on the hood and bent one of the windshield wipers. I'm wondering what I should do—I mean, about insurance. Should I file a police report?"

"I can take an incident report," I replied.

This time, he glanced at the other man, then back to me. He seemed to have something else on his mind.

"Isn't this your security, your bodyguard?" I said, indicating the other person, who looked in shape.

"No, this is Jerry Worms. He's an old school friend from New Jersey."

"Oh, okay. Well, you know as famous as you are, maybe when it's Christmas time and you're around crowds, you should have somebody with you to prevent this."

After pondering my suggestion, he said, "Maybe you're right. Can you recommend anybody?"

"Sure." I handed him my card. "I'm already doing private security on the side. In addition to being a police officer, I own a local karate school."

He studied my card and then looked up. "Why don't you write me a brief resume and bring it out to my ranch?"

I knew that he lived north of Santa Barbara in neighboring Tajiguas Ranch.

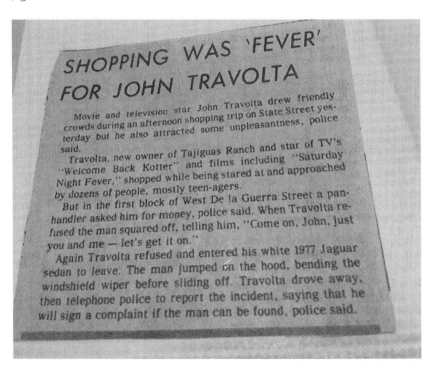

SHOPPING WAS 'FEVER' FOR JOHN TRAVOLTA

Movie and television star John Travolta drew friendly crowds during an afternoon shopping trip on State Street yesterday but he also attracted some unpleasantness, police said.

Travolta, new owner of Tajiguas Ranch and star of TV's "Welcome Back Kotter" and films including "Saturday Night Fever," shopped while being stared at and approached by dozens of people, mostly teen-agers.

But in the first block of West De la Guerra Street a panhandler asked him for money, police said. When Travolta refused the man squared off, telling him, "Come on, John, just you and me — let's get it on."

Again Travolta refused and entered his white 1977 Jaguar sedan to leave. The man jumped on the hood, bending the windshield wiper before sliding off. Travolta drove away, then telephone police to report the incident, saying that he will sign a complaint if the man can be found, police said.

"You're kidding, right?"

"No, I'm not. Drop it off with my housekeeper Rena, and I'll take a look at it."

"Okay."

My sister's fiancé, Rick Hardin, who was in law school, helped me put together a resume. I dropped it off at John's ranch, as I was instructed to do. A year went by and I didn't hear back from John. I figured either he didn't like my resume or his offer was typical Hollywood BS.

After I'd worked as a cop for nearly three years, word filtered back to my commander that I was becoming disenchanted. Worried that I might quit, in late 1977, my commander offered to transfer me to motors, which meant I would be a motorcycle cop.

Riding motors has always been an elite position in the Santa Barbara Police Department. Because a slot only became available if a motorcycle cop retired or died, I jumped at the opportunity. It would be a huge improvement over driving a patrol car. Besides wearing a uniform that featured pants with a stripe and high riding boots, I wore a helmet and even had a special badge. Best of all, unlike patrol officers, I took my motorcycle home after work. It was like my horse.

I rode with a partner, whose name was Sandy Willett. He was "Mary 3" and I was "Mary 4" (Motorcycle 3, and Motorcycle 4). Our beat was the whole city. Our main job was traffic that included responding to accidents and enforcing the traffic laws. In addition, we were allowed to respond to any hot call that came over the radio. We rode ten-hour shifts four days a week, and our beat was the entire city. Unlike patrol officers, we had total freedom.

Sandy and I were so efficient riding together as a team that the rubber handle grips on our motorcycles had to be changed every few months because they were constantly hitting each other. Sandy would think left, and I'd move left.

Since my time with Kim Kahana, I hadn't forgotten about my

interest in doing stunt work. One day in the summer of 1978, I read in the local newspaper that a film company would be doing a location shoot at the Santa Barbara Mission. The film was *The End* and starred Burt Reynolds. Because this would draw a huge crowd of onlookers, I knew the company would be requesting law enforcement traffic control and made a point of making sure I was part of it.

This would be a great opportunity for me to hustle the film's stunt coordinator, Hal Needham, who I learned was Reynolds's best friend. Hustling is what stunt people call introducing themselves to a stunt coordinator. The idea is to introduce yourself, give the coordinator your picture, hopefully shake his hand in order to put a face with the picture, and then leave.

Mary 3 and 4.

Hal Needham wasn't an average stuntman. In 1978, he was the highest paid stuntman in the world. At that time, his career included work on 4,000 television episodes and 300 feature films. Needham wrecked hundreds of cars, fell from tall buildings, got blown up, was dragged by horses, rescued the cast and crew from a Russian invasion in Czechoslovakia, set a world record for a boat stunt on *Gator* (1976), jumped a rocket powered pick-up truck across a canal for a GM commercial, and was the first human to test the car airbag.

On the first day of the location shoot, I worked traffic on my motorcycle, and then during the lunch break approached Hal. I had removed my helmet, which I held under my arm. "Hello, Mr. Needham, my name is Rick Avery."

Hal's eyes seemed to linger for a while on my uniform, then he looked directly at me.

"You working traffic?"

"Yes, sir."

"How long you been a policeman?"

"A little over three years, started on patrol and now work as a motor cop."

"What'd you ride?"

"Kawasaki 900."

"Good ride. Anyway, what can I do for you?"

"I just wanted to meet you to see if you had any stunt work. I live here locally."

"No, Stan Barrett's the only guy I have on this. We got a little gag here. But no, there's nothing on it, but thanks for coming by." (The term "gag" is a holdover from the early silent film days when comedians did slapstick routines that were very physical and called "gags").

"Sure. Nice meeting you." That was it—my one-minute hustle of the great Hal Needham.

The next day, I was again working traffic when the company's production assistant (PA) walked up to me. "Excuse me, are you Rick Avery?"

"Yes."

The PA handed me his radio. "Mr. Needham wants to speak with you."

I took the radio and spoke into it. "This is Rick Avery."

"Rick, Hal Needham," the voice buzzed over the radio. "We met yesterday. Can you change your wardrobe and lead a funeral procession on your motorcycle?"

What a great serendipitous moment. Not only did I get to become reacquainted with Hal Needham and appear in my first Hollywood movie, but was introduced to one of the biggest stars in Hollywood at that time—Burt Reynolds.

At the end of the day, as the company was preparing to leave, Hal said to me, "You're all right, Rick. I like you. Why don't you come down to Hollywood to the Stunts Unlimited office and let's talk?"

Stunt folk are members of the Screen Actors Guild (SAG) and AFTRA unions. They also have fraternal organizations. In the late 1970s, Stunts Unlimited was the most successful and was headed by Hal Needham.

I didn't know what Hal meant when he told me to come to his office to talk. Most guys who wanted to get into the stunt business would have kept that appointment the next day. But I waited. Perhaps because I was afraid that our meeting wouldn't go anywhere and I'd be disappointed. I later found out from stuntman Alan Gibbs that Hal Needham loved cops.

I finally drove to Hal's office that was furnished in a western motif. Hal's secretary was Andre Gibbs, the wife of Alan Gibbs, who would later become my mentor and a major part of my professional life. The 1977 Hal Needham stunt toy set by Gabriel Toys adorned her desk.

When I met with Hal in his office, he wanted to hear about my life. I told him I was married with two kids, that I was a Santa Barbara cop, and that I owned a karate school and a home in Santa Barbara. After seemingly mulling that over for a while, he told me he would like to help me become a stuntman.

I was speechless. Did I hear correctly? Hal Needham, the founder of Stunts Unlimited, just offered to help me become a stuntman? Of course, I'd been hearing similar drumrolls from Kim Kahana for four years—but this was coming from the Hal Needham.

"Here's the thing, Rick," Hal said, then pointed to a wall where a dozen headshots of stuntmen were displayed. "I've got these guys on the wall. They're all members of Stunts Unlimited. I have to take care of these guys first, but what you need to do, Rick, is go out and motocross with those guys, play golf and go hang out. I'll work you, but I have to work them first. But here's the catch. I won't stand for fence walkers, so you're going to need to get rid of your jobs in Santa Barbara and move your family to Los Angeles, and then I'll help you."

I went home and thought about it in depth. The biggest stuntman in the world and best friend of A-list action star Burt Reynolds just offered me the chance of a lifetime. I was just opening a second karate studio in nearby Goleta and my personal security was doing well. Most aspiring stunt people would have jumped at the chance. I had two young children and I was afraid to sell everything and move to Los Angeles, so I didn't take Hal up on the offer.

Chapter 7:

My Big Hollywood Break

Seemingly from out of nowhere, one day John Travolta's attorney, Fred Gaines, called and said, "Can you come to Los Angeles today? John would like you to be in charge of all his security."

I had no idea why Gaines's call had come from out of the blue, but I wasn't going to ask questions. "Sure," I replied. The next day, I hopped in my '69 Vette and drove to LA, and met John's attorney. During our meeting, I learned that over the past year, John had suffered the losses of his mother and his girlfriend Diana Hyland, who died in his arms from cancer, which explained why I hadn't heard from him.

Of primary concern to Gaines was that I wasn't an opportunist who might take advantage of his client. Over the past couple of years, several former disgruntled employees and associates had threatened to file what turned out to be meritless civil lawsuits naming John as defendant, and the attorney wanted make certain that I had the best of intentions.

PINTO, WINOKUR & PAGANO
CERTIFIED PUBLIC ACCOUNTANTS
1900 AVENUE OF THE STARS, SUITE 1630
LOS ANGELES, CA 90067

(213) 879-8090

NEW YORK OFFICE
60 EAST 42ⁿᵈ STREET
NEW YORK, N.Y. 10017
(212) 687-8090

PLEASE REPLY TO: Los Angeles

April 3, 1980

Mr. Rick Avery
3413 State Street
Santa Barbara, California 93105

Re: John Travolta

Dear Rick:

This is to confirm our telephone conversation yesterday.
As we discussed, you will be furnishing twenty-four-hour-
a-day security service for Mr. Travolta. We will be
making checks payable to you and you in turn will make
the necessary payments to the various people who will be
furnishing this service. We will not withhold any Federal
or State taxes but will furnish you a 1099 at the end of
1980.

If you need any help, please contact me.

Yours truly,

PINTO, WINOKUR & PAGANO

Arnold E. Bernstein

AEB:jm

cc: John Travolta
     Fred Gaines
     Ynez Hope
     Bernard Rosenberg

JT billing letter.

"If you're going to one of those types of people—"

"No," I interrupted. "I'm not like that at all."

Having landed the job, over the next few days, I hired a group of cops to work security at John's ranch during their off days. One of them was Bob Fratilla, who called me from the station when I first met John Travolta. Because of a recent break-in attempt, John wanted a 24/7 patrol around his single-story hacienda that sat on 17 acres.

John's ranch was officially called "Tajiguas Ranch" and was located a few miles north of Santa Barbara in Goleta. In close proximity to the ranch was the 300-member spiritual self-sustaining community of "Sunburst" that was inspired by the teachings of Paramahansa Yogananda, the Indian yogi and founder of the Self-Realization Fellowship. The Sunburst members believed in a holistic lifestyle based on meditation, living from the land, organic farming, and—to some

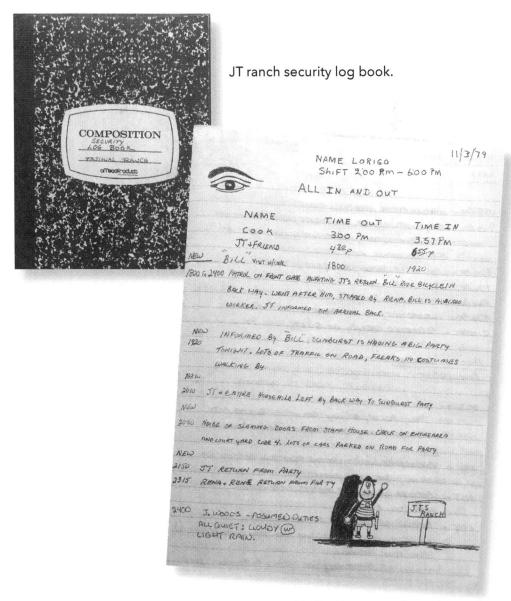

JT ranch security log book.

degree—chastity. Interestingly, John got along well with the Sunburst community and on occasion attended their celebrations.

Over the next two years, besides working as a cop and running my karate school, I continued my security work at John's ranch. Often on weekends, celebrities would come from out of town to spend time with John and enjoy the solitude of his ranch. John was always excited when company was coming, but by far his most prized guest was the legendary James Cagney. In fact, John claimed he was Cagney's greatest fan.

On the afternoon that Mr. Cagney arrived, I had the honor of meeting him. Like John, I was a huge admirer of this legendary Hollywood icon and, as a kid, had watched his movies, many of which are now considered classics. Prior to his arrival, I reflected on the extraordinary energy he exuded on the screen, and in particular his agility. That being said, after briefly meeting him and shaking his frail hand, sadness came over me as I watched him slowly walk away, overweight, and with the help of a cane, as John escorted him into the house. Four years later, Mr. Cagney died from a heart attack.

After I'd known John for some time, he accepted me as a friend and was comfortable with my calling him "JT," which is how his close friends and associates addressed him. I had many memorable times with JT. One morning during the Fourth of July weekend, he called and said, "Come on over and bring the kids. We're having a party with piñatas and everything, and Muhammad Ali's going to be here." My daughter Dianne was nine, and my son Brian was six—both were visiting me from Montana, and any time I had with them was cherished. They were my darlings.

We arrived at the ranch, and when I walked out to the large back patio, I saw Muhammad Ali in conversation with JT. Unbeknownst to me, the heavyweight boxing champ had subtly indicated me and asked JT who's that? At the time, I was into serious bodybuilding. I

Muhammad Ali and me trading uppercuts.

weighed 185 pounds of practically pure muscle and was wearing a Gold's Gym T-shirt. John told him I was his security guy.

The next thing I knew, Muhammad Ali broke away from JT and started walking toward me. The look on his face was menacing, and he seemed to be sizing me up as he continued toward me. I thought to myself *what is he doing?* Seconds later, he arrived in front of me, and without a word grabbed me around my neck and started playfully tussling with me, all the while mumbling under his breath, "So how you doing, Rick? You're John's guy, huh?"

Throughout the rest of the afternoon and evening, Muhammad Ali was an extraordinarily gracious and kind gentleman. He came behind me and took his thumb and index finger and made that little cricket noise in my ear. I turned around and it was Ali messing with me. He played with the kids, told them stories, and did magic tricks. He was fantastic. When it came to meeting celebrities, meeting Muhammad Ali was one of the greatest moments in my life.

One night I was at the ranch watching TV in the kitchen with Rena. We were watching *The Mike Douglas Show,* and the main guest was the stuntman Hal Needham, whom I'd met earlier at the Santa Barbara Mission during the filming of *The End.* On the show, Hal was seen doing a transfer from an airplane to a horse. I said to Rena, "That's what I've been trying to do for a couple of years." Rena and I talked a bit about my lack of success getting into the stunt business, and the conversation ended.

A couple nights later, I was at the ranch and Rena said that JT wanted to talk to me. I met JT and we took a walk while he smoked a cigar after dinner. Following a minute of small talk, he said, "I don't like your being a policeman. It's too dangerous."

"I've been a cop for several years and I've survived just about everything," I responded, lost as to what he was getting to.

He looked at me for a long while, and then asked, "How come you didn't tell me that you wanted to become a stuntman?"

"How did you . . .? Ah, Rena."

"Yes, she mentioned it."

"Well, I don't know. I didn't want to give the impression that I was using you." I never forgot the warning I got from JT's attorney about taking advantage of his client.

"But that's what Hollywood's about," JT said. "We all sort of agree to use each other."

"I guess I'm not built that way. I didn't want to do that."

"I see." Again, he looked at me for a long moment, then continued. "You look a lot like me, actually you remind me of my father when he was young. I'll tell you what—you'll be my stunt double on all my movies from now on."

I hardly knew how to respond to his extremely generous offer, except to sincerely thank him. To say I was excited over the future prospect of working on a movie with John Travolta would be a vast understatement.

Hal Needham doing a transfer from an airplane to a horse.

Besides managing the security at the ranch, JT wanted me to cover his personal security whenever he attended public events. One such memorable event was when he asked me to accompany him to the 37th Golden Globe Awards, honoring the best in film and television for 1979 that was held in January 1980.

JT was going with Marilu Henner, who was nominated for Best Supporting Actress in a Musical or Comedy Television Series *Taxi*. A year earlier, he had a bad incident at the Golden Globes when his driver punched a pushy member of the paparazzi in the face.

I rode with JT and Marilu Henner in JT's limo, and when we arrived at the Golden Globes, before we got out of the limo, JT said to me, "Please don't punch anyone in the mouth."

"Okay, this will be a nice quiet year this year," I replied with a smile.

Being backstage that night at the Golden Globes was one of the most unforgettable nights of my life. I was completely spellbound. Each time I turned around, I was looking at another famous movie star, including Dustin Hoffman, Al Pacino, Dudley Moore, Jane Fonda, Sally Field, Julie Andrews, Peter Sellers, and Jack Lemmon. That year *Kramer vs. Kramer* received the most awards, winning Best Picture, Best Actor in a Drama (Dustin Hoffman), Best Supporting Actress (Meryl Streep), and Best Screenplay (Robert Benton).

Afterwards, we went out to one of Hollywood's historic landmarks, The Brown Derby restaurant, for dessert. Joining JT and Marilu Henner were Jack Lemmon, who was nominated for a Golden Globe for his role in *The China Syndrome*, and 007's Roger Moore, who won the Golden Globe for World Film Favorite. I was sitting at a table off to the side and heard Jack Lemmon say to JT, "Who's that?" as he indicated me.

JT replied, "That's Rick Avery. He's my security."

Lemmon smiled at me and motioned, "Come over here and sit with us and try some of this cake," which I thought was great. I was pinching myself over the next hour. I could hardly believe where I was and the company I was in.

A month later, JT traveled to Philadelphia to star in a mystery thriller called *Blow Out*.

I knew about the film and hadn't heard from anyone, so I figured his earlier promise to include me in his next film was just another hollow promise that I soon got over. I still had my jobs as a cop and karate instructor.

Then about a week later, my home phone rang and a voice on the other end said, "Hello, my name's Freddy Caruso. I'm the executive producer on the film John Travolta is about to begin shooting. I understand you're his stuntman."

I was temporarily speechless. Did he say stuntman? JT had told me that I'd be his stunt double, not his stuntman. Now that I thought about it, was there a difference? "Yes, that's correct," I said in a rapid voice, hoping the producer didn't catch my slow response time.

"Great. Are you available to come out to Philadelphia this weekend?"

"Sure, for how long?"

"Three and a half months."

Whoa! I thought, I'm a fully employed policeman, and I've got a karate school to run. "Can I call you back?" I replied, knowing I needed time to think.

"I'll be here until five."

I hung up and told Joni about the job offer in Philadelphia. She was all for it and assured me she could help take care of the school while I was away. She was extremely competent and a wizard at thinking on her feet. I thanked her and called my watch commander, Lt. Strong, and said, "I've got a question. Can I get a leave of absence for a few months and then come back and continue?"

"What for?" Lt. Strong replied.

"I've been offered the job of being John Travolta's stunt double."

Although the lieutenant was excited about my golden opportunity, there was a problem. "No, you can't," he said. "Santa Barbara PD doesn't give leave of absences. But what I can do to get around it is, you quit, and then when you return from your movie job, we'll rehire you."

"Really?"

"Sure, I don't see a problem with it."

I had an excellent track record with the police department, and I was grateful that they recognized this and cut me some slack.

When I traveled to Philadelphia, besides a handful of military flights when I served in the Army, my only flying experience was in a small Cessna flown by my cousin Frankie Campbell, who was one

Carey Loftin.

of the 25 foster children raised by my Auntie Rose. Frankie and I used to play together back in Peekskill, and he later became a naval aviator. All of a sudden, I'm flying first class along with a couple dozen well-established movie people, including stuntmen Chuck Waters and May Boss, as well as the film's stunt coordinator, 67-year-old Carey Loftin, who was arguably the greatest stunt driver ever and was best known for driving Steve McQueen's car in *Bullet*.

After we landed in Philadelphia and I checked into my suite at the luxurious Plaza Hotel, I was told to report to the stages because Carey Loftin wanted to meet with the stunt people. An hour later, I arrived at the stages and was handed an envelope that contained $250 in cash, which I was told was my weekly per diem for incidental expenses such as bar tabs after work and dry cleaning and such. I was amazed because this per diem amounted to more than half of my weekly salary as a police officer.

Next I was handed a standard weekly stunt contract that stated

I would be paid $1,025 per week. I just traveled across the country in first class, checked into an extravagant hotel suite, and now I've learned that I'll be making over $5,000 per month, plus residuals. Somebody please throw a pail of cold water on me before I pass out! God only knows what I'm expected to do to earn this record-smashing windfall.

The first stunt sequence of *Blow Out* was JT driving a jeep through a Liberty Parade in downtown Philadelphia's Penn Square. He then proceeds up the steps of City Hall and roars into an open courtyard. Carey Loftin handed out various assignments to the stunt guys and then sent them back to the hotel. I sat on a chair by myself as Carey walked over to me and said, "I understand you're John's stunt double."

I was relieved that he hadn't forgotten me, although again a bit concerned by my title of stunt double. It was too late to ask for a clarification.

"Yes, sir," I said, trying to appear eager and confident.

"Okay, I'll tell you what. Let's go down the road. There's a parking lot down there, and we'll check the jeep out."

I made sure when I exited the lot from the stages to use the turn signals and adjust my mirror. I drove safely to the next parking lot, drove around for a couple of minutes, and then pulled into a parking space.

Carey looked over and gave me an incredulous look and said, "Okay."

What I later found out was that what Carey wanted me to do was demonstrate my stunt driving skills by putting the jeep through its paces, which would also let him know if the jeep needed any adjustments. I didn't do any of that. Instead, I drove around the parking lot like I was at the DMV trying to renew my driver's license.

Following Carey's incredulous look, he mentioned that the following day I might have to throw a 90, which is a sudden 90-degree turn that usually results in the vehicle's tires smoking. Oh my God! I knew exactly what Carey meant, but I was worried—petrified would be a better word—because I hadn't been trained as a stunt driver. I was a drag racer and sped around Santa Barbara doing police car chases—and there's a big difference.

When I got back to the hotel, I immediately called Kim Kahana in Chatsworth and told him my predicament. "Kim, what if he asks me to do a 90? I don't know how to do a 90!"

With no other choice, Kim began teaching me over the phone. "The way you throw a 90 is you hit the E-brake and spin the wheel in the direction you want the car's hood to face. Depending on how you want to stop, and how you want the tires turned, you tromp on the brake at the precise moment that . . ." He's telling me this while I'm practicing steering an imaginary steering wheel, grabbing an imaginary emergency brake, and tromping my foot on the hotel carpet, which is where my imaginary brake is located. None of it felt good to me.

The next morning, I arrived at the set and reported to hair and wardrobe where I was fitted with a wig matching JT's hair and an identical blue coat that he would be wearing in the shot. While I was there, I noticed a guy dressed just like me. He had the same wig and coat that I had as if he was JT's double.

I suddenly had a sinking feeling. This was all too reminiscent of my childhood in East Bronx when I was always the last kid chosen because no one thought I had whatever it took. Somebody better qualified was going to end up being JT's stunt double. I feared that my inadequacy had once again caught up to me.

Trying to keep my head up, I walked over to the Liberty Parade staging to find a thousand extras milling about. They were all local citizens who were unaccustomed to being around Hollywood movie people.

I spotted a couple of stunt guys from the plane. They were dressed as policemen and sat on horses. I could tell they were real cowboys. I later found out they were sitting on highly-trained stunt horses that had been transported to Philadelphia specifically for work in the film. These two horses were situated at the top of two flights of stairs where the jeep was supposed to drive up and then proceed on into the courtyard.

When I walked over to those stairs, I was joined by Carey, who casually mentioned that there was only four inches of clearance, two inches on each side, for the jeep to fit through. "I'm going to let you drive the rehearsal," Carey said. "To be honest, I wasn't impressed yesterday. If you don't do well in the rehearsal, Chuck is dressed like John and he'll take over."

So that was the other guy I saw earlier in wardrobe dressed as JT. I suddenly became an agonizing mix of depression and anxiety. I'd never felt so much responsibility. The film's director was the acclaimed Brian De Palma, the director of photography was the award-winning Vilmos Zsigmond, and MGM Studios had put up the $18-million budget (and those were 1980 dollars). On top of all this, I was about to be called on to perform the rehearsal in front of 1,000 extras.

"Okay, fair enough," I replied, and then slipped in behind the wheel of the jeep. All too quickly, everyone was in position and someone yelled, "Action!" I stomped on the gas and heard the powerful engine roar to life. An instant later, the jeep slammed into the stairs and I found myself looking through the windshield to the sky, convinced the jeep was going to loop over and land on its roof. But instead, it came crashing down onto the lower flight of stairs, and then rocketed in midair onto the upper flight. Because my foot was frozen on the gas, the jeep's back wheels kept spinning. When I hit the top landing, I slammed on the brakes because I was scared to death. The jeep's front hit ground with a loud thud, which caused one of the horses to rear, sending people running in all directions. This wasn't a half-speed rehearsal. This was a crazed stunt guy wannabe trying not

to look stupid. As the dust settled and the screams died down, I was convinced that I'd be on a plane that night and back on my police motorcycle in the morning, never again to hear from John Travolta or anyone else in the Hollywood film industry.

Just then, I looked in jeep's left side view mirror and saw this red-faced old man running toward the jeep. It was Carey Loftin. He was approaching 66 years of age and shouldn't have been running. He didn't look happy. Arriving at the driver's door, he reached in through the open window, grabbed me by my coat and yelled, "That was great, kid! Can you do that again?!"

"I . . . I . . ." was all I could utter. As Carey walked away, for the first time I heard the growing applause that was coming from the hundreds of onlookers. In front of me, sitting on one of the horses, a seasoned stuntman gave me a subtle nod of approval. This jeep sequence marked the beginning of my stunt career. Ironically, I had become a hero totally by accident.

Doubling JT again.

After being in the negative job of a police officer where I wasn't happy, suddenly extras and looky-loos were asking to take a photograph with me and wanting my autograph. At the end of each take, they'd come over and slap my back and tell me how great I was and ask me to tell them about John Travolta. I was in heaven. This surely wasn't the Philadelphia that W.C. Fields loathed throughout his career and once remarked, "I once spent a year in Philadelphia. I think it was on a Sunday."

At the end of the day, I signed a few more autographs, and then changed my clothes and decided to take a walk around the city. I remember walking in my civilian clothes and when I turned the corner a block away, suddenly nobody knew me. This was a great lesson about being a stuntman. When all is said and done, John Travolta will always be remembered as the one who drove that jeep throughout the entire chase sequence because he'd done the isolated close-ups.

Since the early westerns, the stuntmen who double for these stars have been the unsung heroes of the Hollywood movie industry. Maybe this is part of what JT meant when he told me that in Hollywood we all agree to use each other.

When I returned to the hotel, I walked into my room and grabbed two newspapers that were routinely delivered to my suite. While jumping up and down on the bed, I threw those newspapers all around the room while shouting with glee. When I finished, I called Joni and told her what a remarkable day I'd had. She could instantly tell that I had undergone a major change. And she was right. For the first time in my life, I felt totally validated. I had finally received the recognition I had so desperately sought.

Besides working as JT's stuntman, I served as his double and stand-in. I'm five-seven, JT's six foot. The actor and his double are supposed to be the same height or close to it. Because JT was much taller, I stood on apple crates when I stood in for lighting and camera moves. Eventually, the wardrobe department came up with a pair of shoes with four-inch lifts. I looked like Frankenstein when I showed up wearing those shoes.

The director of photography, Vilmos Zsigmond, would sometimes take hours to light a particular sequence. Although I appeared to be standing there like a frozen mannequin, I was taking it all in and getting an education in filmmaking.

Over the next three months, I learned what everyone did on the set and the terminology they used. Had I paid for this education in college as a film major, it would have cost me tens of thousands of dollars and taken five times as long. Instead, I received a better education in a fraction of the time from key grips like Dicky Deats, plus MGM paid me five grand a month plus three months of lavish living at the Plaza Hotel. (As a footnote to readers of this book who are film buffs, during the editing process of *Blow Out*, two reels of footage from the Liberty Parade sequence were stolen and were never to be seen again. Because of this, the scenes had to be reshot at a cost of

JT and I returning from *Blow Out* in his jet.

John Travolta

March 1985

Letter of recommendation for Rick Avery.

To whom it may concern:

I first used Rick Avery on a film I did called "Blow Out".It was his first film and he impressed everyone.He was thrown into advanced stunts on his first day and came through with flying colors.

I used him on three more of my films,and to the best of my knowledge he has been used on many films since then.

He has a great personality,is easy to work with, and will get the job done,

Yours truly,

John Travolta

$750,000. Perhaps selfishly, I was happy to hear when it happened because I made another weekend of work).

When I returned from *Blow Out*, I wasn't the same person who had left Santa Barbara three months earlier. I wasn't a street guy anymore. In a sense, I was now looking at life through a different set of eyes.

A few days after my return, I walked into the police department where my lieutenant greeted me with a warm smile. "Welcome back, Rick! How was it? You ready to come back? I can have the paperwork ready by tomorrow."

"I'm not coming back," I replied calmly. "I've got a new life."

The lieutenant was visibly let down.

"But we've got you a new motorcycle. It's in the crate down at the city yard."

I'd been begging for the new Kawasaki 1000. I was always riding the 900 and everybody else had a new bike. It was clear that the lieutenant was trying to tempt me. Besides the new bike, we both knew that motorcycle cops in Santa Barbara are a lifetime position that comes with a great pension. But I'd already made up my mind and thanked the lieutenant for his offer and for everything he'd done for me while I was a cop.

One day, Joni and I stopped to eat at a Taco Bell in Los Angeles where I unintentionally ended up proposing, at least at that particular time and place. For a long time, I'd carried a black bank pouch that contained all my important papers from my karate school. When we exited our car, I routinely took that pouch with me inside the Taco Bell.

I'd forgotten that Joni's engagement ring was in that pouch, and so when I prepared to pay the bill, she spotted the ring. There was no way I was going to convince her that she hadn't seen a diamond ring or that, if she had, that it wasn't hers. So with as much fanfare as I could muster up sitting at a table at a Taco Bell, I proposed and Joni accepted. While not the most romantic setting, we were both thrilled.

Joni and I were married in Santa Barbara on October 24, 1981. My two best men were Scott Mitchell and my police motorcycle partner Sandy Willett. Our wedding was a major police event. Strings of tin cans tied to the rear bumper of our limo made a huge racket as we drove down the main street in Santa Barbara and circled the police station several times during its change of watch. Astonished officers loading cars with shotguns couldn't believe their eyes.

Married.

Picking up our police escort, we drove to the airport where we took off for Las Vegas. When the plane lifted off the runway, Joni and I looked out the window and, at 500 feet below, saw all the guys from our wedding party lying on an adjacent taxi-way, their pants pulled down to their knees and their bare butts sticking up in a grand send-off. No one was about to say anything regarding this risqué display because all the participants were cops.

As a footnote, I was recently at the Santa Barbara Airport, and a gentleman approached me asking if I was Rick Avery. He remembered the fanfare that had occurred 35 years earlier at the airport — butts and all!

Chapter 8:

Breaking into the Business

After making all this fantastic money on *Blow Out* and being convinced that my stunt career was going to take off, over the next year and a half, I was hired for only two minor jobs. All I was doing was working at the karate school and thinking that maybe I should have never quit the Santa Barbara Police Department, which caused me to lose my pension.

Then out of the blue, Tom Elliot called. I initially met Tom at Kim Kahana's Stunt School and we hit it off well. Tom had recently got his SAG card and broken into the stunt business. Because he knew I wasn't getting much work, he suggested that I drive to Santa Ynez, which is ten miles north of Santa Barbara, and meet Alan Gibbs.

Alan was a protégé and good friends with Hal Needham and was working as a stuntman on the film shoot *The Postman Always Rings Twice* starring Jack Nicolson and Jessica Lange. In fact, Alan had been Jack Nicolson's stunt double for quite a while.

The following day, I arrived at the location and milled around in the background, shaking a few hands and having a coffee at craft service. Then out of nowhere, a big yellow Cadillac El Dorado pulled onto the set, and behind the wheel sat Alan Gibbs. He looked decidedly Hollywood with his shirt collar turned up and wearing rose-colored Ray-ban sunglasses and sporting a Stetson buffalo nickel hat.

Fifteen minutes later, Tom Elliot introduced me to Alan, who in later years was considered by many to have been one of the best stuntmen to ever don a pad. Alan was eight years older than I was, stood five feet-nine and spoke with a gruff, gravelly voice that was the result of years of chain-smoking. During our brief meeting, I did my basic hustle and thanked him for his time. When he walked away, my general impression of him was that he was the consummate man's man. Alan had the reputation of liking quiet, humble, appreciative people, which had always been my basic personality.

When I broke into the stunt business in the early 1980s, on the job training was the best way to learn to be a stuntman. Initially, a person came in with a single talent, and they were usually at the top at their game, such as motocross, race car driving, or gymnastics. When I met Alan, I was a motorcyclist, black belt tournament competitor, and a fairly decent drag race driver. Apparently, Alan put those things together and felt that he could build on that. I could fight, but Alan had to teach me how to do a picture fight. I could drag race, but as a stuntman I had to be taught basic car work. I had some skills and work ethic behind a voracious desire to learn my new craft.

The year was 1982 and I hadn't heard from Alan or any of his stunt buddies for months. I hadn't worked in the movie business for well over a year, and for all intents and purposes had no real contacts. I was still living in Santa Barbara, which had been the problem with my martial arts and stunt careers. Los Angeles was the epicenter of both, and I was still considered an outsider.

Then I again received a call from Tom Elliot, who said, "How would you like to come to LA and join a stunt association that's being put together by Alan Gibbs?"

Did I hear him correctly? I asked him to repeat what he just said, and he repeated the same question. Before he reached the end of his sentence, I replied, "Yes, yes, yes, yes, and yes!"

The entire stuntman's community was furious with Alan for forming International Stunts Association (ISA). Alan didn't walk out with anybody from Stunts Unlimited—he walked out by himself and with big plans. He wanted his newly-formed association to be worldwide with offices in London and France and was considering allowing women to join, which no Hollywood stunt organization had done. Not only did Alan start ISA after leaving Stunts Unlimited, but he put its main office in the same building and on the floor right below Stunts Unlimited.

When I arrived, the only people that I knew were Alan, Richard Epper, and Tom Elliot. I later found out that Richard and Tom were a special part of Alan's inner circle.

Early one morning, Alan called and said, "Rent a car and come to LA. We're going out to Indian Dunes near Six Flags where we all motocross. There's an abandoned airport strip out there, and I'll teach you how to drive a car and how to do one-eighties and nineties."

The airport at Indian Dunes was built by the Newhall Land & Farming Company. Although the strip and hangar were for the corporation's aircraft, in the late 1970s and early 1980s the area was used for filming *The Black Sheep Squadron* TV series and many other films and TV shows.

Within the hour, I rented a Chevy Camaro from a local car rental concern and hot footed it to Indian Dunes where I met up with Alan. Throughout the day, Alan and I put that Camaro through what was undoubtedly its worst rental experience. We burned the tires, redlined the RPMs, and pushed its suspension and transmission far beyond what the manufacturer had envisioned in the car's basic design.

Alan taught me how to do 90-degree, 180-degree, and reverse 180-degree slides and turns. He taught me how to use the emergency brake to lock up the rear tires, tricks for hitting a mark consistently, and how to do power slides while remaining in control at all times.

There are teachers, and there are teachers. Certain men can demonstrate how to do something in the simplest way so that the student picks it up quickly. Alan had that knack. He said he could teach an 80-year-old woman to do stunts. He would say, "Rick, stunts is all kid shit."

Years later, I was setting up the stunts for the WaterWorld show at Universal Studios in Hollywood. Lots of new stunt recruits for that show, who are now veteran stunt people, were included.

I used Alan's simplest teaching method for them to teach fights, high falls, and fires. The star was a 5-time Jet Ski champion Larry Rippenkroeger. This was back when jet skis were stand up. To prove my point of being taught by "the best," "simplistically," Larry took me out during a lunch break when we were training at Lake Castaic and taught me to stand up and rudimentary basics. I later got Larry his job as Bruce Willis's stunt double.

Late that afternoon when I brought the car back to the car rental place, as soon as I pulled in, a tire went flat. I stepped on the E-brake and it broke off. The radiator was already overheating and suddenly began belching steam from under the hood. As I got out of the car, the young rental agent arrived with a bewildered expression on his face. "What happened?"

"I don't know," I replied as I slammed the car door. "But if this is the kind of crap you guys rent out, I'm never coming back here again!"

After apologizing profusely, the young agent refunded the car's rental cost and gave me a complimentary two-day car rental that was good for a year. God, how I miss the good old days when there was service.

I'd ridden motorcycles since I was a teenager, but I'd never ridden a dirt bike until Alan called one day and said, "Richard Epper and I are going to go ride bikes. You want to go?"

"Sure," I replied eagerly. "Let me find my tennis shoes and . . ."

"Forget the tennies, Rick. We're riding in dirt. You wear tennis shoes and you'll break your ankles. I've got some gear you can use."

An hour later, I met Alan and Richard at Indian Dunes that had three motocross courses. Alan brought with him a motocross outfit for me to wear that included boots, a helmet, gloves, and goggles. He also brought a 250cc Suzuki for me to ride. It had just rained, and the courses were wet, which is ideal for motocross.

For the entire afternoon, Alan and Richard taught me the essentials of motocross racing. Later, I had the joy of riding with them at Judo Gene LeBell's place in Frazier Park. I took to motocross with the same intense enthusiasm as when Scott Mitchell introduced me to surfing. When I came home to Santa Barbara, I was still wearing the

My new bike.

clothes that were given to me by Alan, only now they were covered with mud. When Joni saw my mud encrusted face, she said, "My God, what happened to you?!"

"I fell in love with motocross, that's what happened to me. And I'm buying a motocross bike tomorrow!" which I did.

There was no limit to what Alan Gibbs could teach me. One day, he took a group of us to Hanson Dam. We were there specifically for Alan to show us how to teach a horse to be a fall horse and to rig a "step" to do saddle falls.

Initially, I thought it would take Alan the better part of the day, but it took him less than 20 minutes. Alan haltered the horse, tied up one of its front legs so that the horse was standing on only three legs, and then maneuvered the animal in such a way that it had no choice but to fall in the sand. Later that afternoon, Alan taught us how to do saddle falls without getting hurt, which he did in less than an hour. He was a simplistic teaching master.

Opposite: Alan Gibbs taught me everything about doing saddle falls. On the right, the Master in action.

One of many aspects that made Alan unique as a stuntman was that he could get a director to bite on anything Alan wanted to do because he demonstrated it so well. In 1975, Alan was hired as a stunt coordinator on *One Flew over the Cuckoo's Nest* that starred Jack Nicolson. One afternoon, he accompanied the film's director, Milos Forman, and the director of photography to scout locations and ended up at the mental hospital that was central to the picture. In discussing the scene in which Nicolson (R.P. McMurphy) escapes from the hospital and then commandeers a school bus and takes the patients fishing, Forman said to Alan, "How would you escape from this hospital? It's surrounded by this high fence and all this barb wire."

Alan glanced at the fence and surrounding area and then casually replied, "I'd just climb the barb wire fence and then jump onto that tree on the other side and then drop to the ground."

Milos gave Alan an incredulous look. "I don't think that's

possible. That's a fifteen-foot fence and even if you could get to the top, that barb wire—"

Alan interrupted. "I'll show you." Over the next two minutes, he climbed to the top of the 15-foot fence, then skillfully worked his way through the maze of razor-sharp barb wire, and then leapt eight feet in the air onto an adjacent tree branch. After playfully dangling for a few moments in midair, he then dropped to the ground. Alan did exactly what he said he would do (he reenacted the same escape in the movie), although he tore his hands up pretty good in the process.

Alan loved teaching anyone who wanted to learn, and his teaching wasn't limited to stunt work. For example, one morning he called and said, "Come over to my place, Rick, and I'll teach you how to pour cement. I'm building a block wall at my driveway and putting new windows in my house. You want to learn how to put a new window in your house, Rick?" Alan didn't only do this with me. I wasn't singled out. He did this with a dozen guys.

When Alan first formed ISA, the guys he brought together were either relative unknowns like me or bag carrying stuntmen who hadn't worked in a long time. Alan took me in strictly on the recommendation of Tom Elliot, to whom I am forever grateful for his help and friendship.

We started in an empty office. Everybody brought in their 8X10s and we paneled the walls like the inside of a barn and began having meetings. There was a huge risk in forming this renegade stunt association. Many of us were fearful of being permanently ostracized from the stuntman's community if our association failed. The membership of Stunts Unlimited called us "The Muppets" and now and again commented that none of us would work for a long time, if, in fact, we ever worked again.

The way the stunt business works is a stunt coordinator supplies the work. If a stunt person doesn't know any stunt coordinators, they'll never get a job. Alan told us, "Besides me, there's no other coordinator in here now, but I'll guarantee you, you'll all be coordinators someday." The insight and confidence of this man never stopped. As a footnote, decades later, all but a few of us had become stunt coordinators.

At first we had no work, and then I got a call from Freddy Caruso, with whom I'd done *Blow Out* with John Travolta. "I'm doing a picture in Philadelphia called *Fighting Back*," he said. "Can you come out and coordinate it?" The movie was an action, crime drama starring Tom Skerritt and Patti LuPone.

"I can't," I said, disappointed. "I don't know anything about stunt coordinating, but I have Alan Gibbs here and he can coordinate it."

Alan agreed to do the show and was hired as both a second unit

Alan setting up shot.

Fighting Back - top, me with Eurlyne Epper and Alan Gibbs. Middle on the left, me, Jack Gill and Tom Elliot, and on the right, Brian Smrz and Jophrey Brown; on the left, that's me doing some kicking in a bar fight.

director and stunt coordinator. Best of all, the majority of ISA's previously out of work stuntmen were suddenly gainfully employed. I felt good because I had immediately contributed something to Alan's newly-formed stuntmen's organization.

ᔯ ᔯ ᔯ

What I've thoroughly loved about working in the Hollywood film and television industry for all these years is that every film and television show presents a different array of situations and colorful characters. Whoever came up with the line "You can't make this stuff up" must have been referring to the grand stage of Hollywood.

Many filmgoers readily recall the highly successful (1981) *The Cannonball Run* action/comedy movie that featured Burt Reynolds and a group of characters racing across the country in various cars and trucks.

When in 1984 *Cannonball Run II* was about to go into production, Alan called and said, "I'm going to have you out on Cannonball Run two, and I need you to do me a favor. I need a bodyguard for Jackie Chan, who's working on the movie."

Legendary stuntman/director Hal Needham.

With Jackie Chan and Mike Fitzmorris.

Apparently Jackie Chan was supposed to do a movie for the triads back in Hong Kong, and he came to the United States instead to make the sequel to the first Cannonball Run. This was what kung-fu icon Bruce Lee did decades earlier when he stiffed the Chinese triad who controlled Hong Kong's film industry to come to the United States to pursue his film career. Ironically, both Lee's hit movie *Enter the Dragon* and the Cannonball Run movies were produced by Hong Kong producer Raymond Chow.

"So I'm to be a bodyguard?" I replied, surprised.

"No, you're doing stunts. I need you to find me one."

I was relieved. I'd rather crash a dozen cars per day than be constantly looking over my shoulder for members of the Chinese triad.

"Mike Fitzmorris," I said, instantly coming up with the name. "He's a former cop who just retired. Mike's great because he's six foot, strong, and can carry a gun. He'll smile all the time, but if someone needs to be put down, he'll be fast and diplomatic."

Doubling for
Dean Martin,
Dom Deluise
and Sammy
Davis, Jr.

All in a day's work on *Cannonball Run II*.

Alan was delighted that I'd found someone and put Mike on a three-month stunt contract. Mike had never seen that much money. He lived with Jackie in Tucson throughout the entire movie. Understandably, Jackie happily paid for everything.

When I arrived on the *Cannonball Run II* set on the first day of shooting, I wasn't expecting to see Hal Needham sitting in the director's chair. I wondered if he still recalled five years earlier when, as a total unknown, I turned down his offer to help me get into the stunt business.

Alan had me do practically everything in this picture. Besides doing two fights with Jackie Chan, I doubled the majority of the actors, including Joe Theismann driving the Monkey Mobile, Captain Chaos (Dom Deluise) driving the Nuke Mobile, Sammy Davis Jr. driving a Corvette, several comedians sitting in a helicopter on the roof of a car speeding through a tunnel, and Dean Martin. In addition, I drove a police car doing near-misses during several multiple-car chase sequences, and a Ferrari being filmed from a helicopter at high speed. I was one busy stuntman!

There was a scene in the movie where I and two other stuntmen got jerked out of a rowboat when Jackie Chan drove a car into a lake. Alan was doubling Abe Vigoda, Clay Boss was doubling Alex Rocco, and I was doubling Sid Caesar. The three of us were holding a fishing pole, and Jackie's car accidently catches our fishing line and, as a result, we get ripped out of the boat.

Just prior to shooting the scene, Alan walked over to me, poked me in the chest, and said, "I guarantee you before we get done with this shot, you'll see Hal, thousand dollar ostrich boots and all, walk into this lake and yell at everyone."

"Really?" I said.

"Yup."

We rehearsed the scene. The camera was focused on me and the other two stuntmen standing in the rowboat tightly holding onto a T-bar that was connected to the fishing pole. This pole connected us to a speedboat that was off camera and was as powerful as a drug runner's boat from *Miami Vice*.

When Hal yelled "Action!" the speedboat's driver pushed the boat's throttle to full speed. The taunt line then pulled me and the other stuntmen out of the rowboat and into the water. We were dragged along the surface for about 50 feet, and then just before I was pulled underwater, I heard Hal yell "Cut!" and when I came up, the first thing I heard was Hal screaming. "What in the fuck was that?! What the fuck are you guys doing?! You driving that fucking boat, when I say action, you stomp on the gas!" I glanced to the source of the yelling, and there was Hal, knee deep in the lake, thousand dollar boots and all, just like Alan had predicted.

Everyone looked at each other dumbfounded. The other stuntmen and I got back into the rowboat, and when Hal yelled "Action!" the speedboat driver shoved that throttle forward so hard and fast that he almost broke it. We were yanked out of that row boat with such force that we were still above the rowboat and parallel to the water

Hold on for dear life.

before we went flying forward. Thank God that was a take because another one of those might have ripped my shoulders from their sockets. Hal just walked away.

Hal had a similar blowup on another movie I was working on. I was behind the wheel of a car that was sitting in a driveway, preparing to peel out into the street. The extremely detail-oriented script gal

Doing a high fall.

walked up to Hal and pointed to my car's driver's side mirror that had broken off in an earlier take and was now hanging loosely. She said, "Hal, that isn't going to match."

This was a sunset shot of cars racing out of the driveway with dust and gravel flying everywhere. Hal knew what viewers saw and what they didn't. He kicked the mirror completely off the car door, and then said to the script gal, "So how's that now?!"

One of the many things that I loved and admired about Alan Gibbs was that when he worked as stunt coordinator, he always supported his stuntmen. One of the best examples occurred on *Cannonball Run II*. There was a scene in which Dean Martin had to step onto a painter's scaffold at night from inside a tenth-floor hotel room. Working as Dean Martin's double, I was having a problem stepping out onto that scaffold because each time I did, it would swing out, and

I was worried that I would fall in between the scaffold and the side of the hotel.

Alan had no fear of heights and said, "Just jump over the sill and onto the scaffold in one move—like this." He then sprung like a cat and easily leapt onto the scaffold. I felt there was no way I could do that. He was patiently helping me work through it my way when the unit production manager's harsh voice came over Alan's radio, "What's the hold up?" I could see that Alan didn't like the man's tone.

"Come up here and I'll show you," he replied.

The man arrived and walked over to Alan and continued wanting to know what was the delay. Alan grabbed him and forced him over to the window where he pushed his head over the sill. "That's what's taking too long. You jump out there!"

My jaw dropped. The production manager nearly wet his pants and looked back at Alan and said sheepishly, "Take as long as you like."

After the man left, Alan said, "Damn producers will challenge a stuntman to do something like a high fall saying, 'I can do that,' knowing no one will ever ask them to! Bastards!"

Alan also always had the backs of the actors he doubled. One night on the set of *Chinatown*, Jack Nicolson purposely stumbled into the L.A. River. It was part of the scene. Alan was Jack's stunt double and became concerned that Jack was in danger of drowning and jumped in to help him. Enraged that Alan had entered the shot, the director, Roman Polanski, chewed him out. Alan never took shit from anyone and got in Polanski's face. "Don't you tell me what my fucking job is! I'll knock you out! My job is to protect him!" Jack loved that, and from that moment on, Jack's directors weren't allowed to send Alan home without first checking with Jack.

Near the end of *Cannonball Run II*, I finally summoned up enough nerve to talk to Hal Needham. I walked over to him and said, "Mr. Needham, I don't know if you remember me, but—"

Legendary stunt crew *Cannonball Run II*.

"I remember you," he interjected, then allowed me to continue.

"Yes, well, I just want to thank you. What you offered me a couple years ago was the world, and I didn't take it. I couldn't take it. I had a wife and family. But I want you to know, I'm here with Alan and I'm doing stunts and it still worked out okay."

He looked at me for a long moment, then a slight smile turned the corners of his mouth and he said, "That's great, kid."

Hal had a unique style and a grand sense of humor. One of his directorial trademarks was showing outtakes during the end credits. On a lighter side, when he began directing, his films were usually blasted by the critics but did well at the box-office. To counter his critics, he once took out an ad in the trade papers quoting his negative reviews, but showing a wheelbarrow filled with money. Unlike

Above, Joni and Mikey. On the left, Dianne and Brian playing with their new baby brother.

the majority of directors, Hal allowed the crew to watch dailies and catered food and an open bar. Although practically unheard of, it was morale boosting.

There came a time when Alan Gibbs said to me almost word for word what Hal Needham had told me in 1978 when I met with him at his office at Stunts Unlimited. "It's time for you to move to L.A., Rick." Alan held up a piece of paper and continued, "I have a job here that starts Monday and a list of guys who need work. You, on the other hand, have a business in Santa Barbara that's doing well and a wife who's contributing to your income. So I'm going to give this job to Clay Boss because he has nothing going but this. He lives here and he drives here and this is his life. Your life is still apart, so why would I give you the job over him? You move to L.A. and I'll double your income in the first year. It's your call."

Fair enough. Over the next month, I sold my home in Santa Barbara and sold my karate school to one of my black belts, Gabe Fabella. A year earlier in February 1985, Joni gave birth to a healthy baby boy, whom we named Mikey, who quickly became the love of our lives.

Joni moved us to Los Angeles to a 1,200 square-foot house in Canoga Park while Alan and I traveled to New York to work on the romantic comedy *Legal Eagles* starring Robert Redford and Debra Winger. To her credit, Joni managed the entire move from Santa Barbara and put together our new home in Canoga Park while taking care of our one-year-old baby.

One night when Joni and I talked on the phone, she asked me to ask Alan about getting her into stunts. When I mentioned this to Alan, he said, "Absolutely fucking not, it'll ruin your marriage!" Needless to say, I wasn't looking forward to telling Joni that when I came home.

Alan started giving me jobs, although at times unnerving. On *Legal Eagles*, he called me to the set one day for a simple car gag. "Rick, all I need for you to do is come flying around that corner and head for this crosswalk and then come to sudden stop—and don't, whatever you do, hit Robert Redford. Can you do that?"

Right. At the time, Robert Redford was a million-dollar actor. Two days later, Alan asked me to throw a 90 up to a person standing between another person and a $100,000 Mercedes—"And whatever you do, don't brush up against either of them, let alone hit them." Eventually, I learned that it wasn't how good a driver I was, but the experience and confidence that I brought to the set. Alan taught me kid shit in baby steps.

The 1970s and 1980s was arguably the golden age for stunts. There was an abundance of television action and drama shows. *Knight Rider, Riptide, The A-Team,* and *Fall Guy* kept a large contingent of stunt folk working multiple shows. Besides stunts, we were often asked to do small acting parts, which technically became another contract. As a result, many stunt people were collecting three and four contracts over a 24 or 48-hour period, in addition to future residuals.

When the studios became aware of the small fortunes being made by stunt people, they put a stop to it by calling us "utility stunts." When this went into effect, whenever stunt people showed up on a set, our contract stipulated that we could play a number of different parts all under one umbrella. Essentially, we became the proverbial Jack of all trades.

Additionally, during this time period, the feature film industry was multi-faceted in a wide spectrum of low-to-high budget films. The low budget feature was a great place for an inexperienced stunt coordinator/second unit director like myself to cut his teeth. When I made mistakes, it didn't hurt me in the big feature arena. I was fortunate to work on many low budgets that led to the higher budget features.

In the beginning of March 1988, Alan was suddenly hospitalized. I was among his close friends who visited him every day. Because he was in considerable pain, his doctor ordered large amounts of morphine. Much of the time, it didn't help, but Alan fought hard. One day, I walked into his hospital room and he was smiling from ear to ear, which I assumed was caused by the morphine. "What're you smiling about?" I asked.

He kept staring at a spot that was directly to my right. "I'm staring at that brilliant blue light. You can't see it?"

"Where? What is it?"

"Right next to you." After a brief pause, he continued, "It's Jesus.

He's standing beside you."

This revelation was coming from a man who if he told me the sky is falling, the sky is falling. Drugs or no drugs, I was convinced that this wasn't bullshit. It suddenly occurred to me that here was a chance to ask Jesus a question. I asked Alan what Jesus was saying.

To this day, Alan's answer sends chills up my spine. He smiled and said, "That's for me to know and for you to find out." How sober does a macho man like Alan have to be to say he was seeing Jesus and that I'd have this same experience when my time came? Alan Gibbs was incapable of lying, and he was a man that I would have followed anywhere.

On March 18, 1988, Alan died from a rare kidney disease. He was only 48 years of age, eight years older than my father, who passed at age 40. Alan used to tell me about every major stunt coordinator on the set, "Don't pay attention to any of these suckers and listen to what I tell you. And what I tell you, you can take to the bank."

Although Alan wasn't old enough to be my father, he became a father figure to me because he gave me everything a son wants and needs. I could have never gotten anywhere in the stunt world without the patient help and guidance of Alan Gibbs, who had my best interest and my back every step of the way.

On his death bed, he called Richard Epper in for a few words, telling Richard he was like a son. He then called Tom Elliot in, telling him the same. He called me in and said I was like a brother to him. That bothered me for an entire year because I also wanted to be like a son to Alan. Now I realize a brother is just as good. I miss Alan every day on every set. I love him.

At the memorial for Alan, Jack Nicolson gave a speech that made us all laugh and cry. While he was giving the oration, someone out in the street was peeling rubber. It was appropriate for Jack to say in his own unique way, "And there he is outside," referring to his loyal stuntman Alan.

Alan Gibbs did stunts with strength, ease, finesse, confidence, and joy, as shown in these photos. He was an all-round stuntman who did it all, and did it a lot. Everything from the biggest cannon roll in history at the time, 100-foot high falls, motorcycle jumps with limited frontend travel, horse work, fights, creative sequence development, rigging (before there were riggers), and every other form of stunts expected from a professional stuntman. One is humbled by this once in a lifetime talent.

In 1988, my son Mikey was three years old. Jack Gill called and asked if Mikey could do some stunt doubling for a gnome puppet in the movie *A Gnome Named Gnorm* for director Stan Winston. Stan was a special effects makeup master who built the model creatures for *Edward Scissorhands*, *Predator*, *Alien*, and *Iron Man*, and won three Academy Awards.

We took Mikey to the stage to see if he would fit in the costume, and when we walked in, the *Alien* and *Predator* costumes were on display. Mikey was in my arms and became scared when he saw these creatures. When we discussed Mikey being a double, he seemed reluctant. Stan Winston asked if he could try something. He went to the head of the robotic gnome that was cute and had big blue eyes. He pretended to be the voice, and when the gnome asked Mikey if

Mikey and a Gnome named Gnorm.

Mikey.

he would be his double, Mikey smiled and gave a vigorous yes. The stunts, of course, were minimal, just being in the costume mostly for movement, and in one scene some small squibs went off after Mikey jumped from a desk.

In that same year, my daughter Dianne moved back to Los Angeles to live with me. For years, she had said she'd move the day after she turned 18. She couldn't wait to get out of Montana. I was overjoyed with the news because I finally got to be with her fulltime.

Meanwhile, Brian remained at Belgrade High School in Montana, having a successful football career. Three years later, I was blessed to have him move in as well after he returned to Santa Barbara for a year to complete his high school education at my alma mater, San Marcos High School. Having Dianne and Brian live with me helped fill the hole left by my years of seeing them sporadically during my visitation rights. I think that to this day they both hold onto their lack of time with me during their childhoods, but this mends a little each year.

My sons Mikey and Brian as my safety team.

Monty Cox is a close friend and the premier Exotic animal trainer in Hollywood, who works with lions, tigers, bears, baboon, and alligators. He called one day and said, "Hey, Ricky, I got a call from a show called *Baywatch*. They're shooting a pilot down at the Queen Mary in Long Beach and they want to have an alligator in the pool for a scene. I want you to come help me as a safety."

"Umm, ah, Monty, I don't know the first thing about alligators."

"You don't have to, Ricky," he continued. "Just show up tomorrow and I'll show you what we have to do. Piece of cake," and hung up.

When I arrived the next day, I met with Monty, who was standing next to an alligator in a cage. The mean-looking reptile hissed angrily as it slammed its tail against the metal with a lot of prehistoric force. For years, I'd called Monty by his real first name Lamont. "So, Lamont, what do you want me to do?"

"Nothing, Ricky. The alligator has his jaw wired shut, so just help me get him in and out of the pool. Just watch for the tail when it swings because it can break your leg."

Hmmmm, I thought, not really the piece of cake, as promised.

We lifted the alligator out of the cage and got it into the pool where it gracefully dove to the deep end. Minutes later, I saw the camera crew in the water jumping out of the pool like popcorn kernels. Monty came over to me and said, "We gotta go in and get the alligator. The wire came off."

"Monty, I don't have any idea how to go about doing that, pal."

"We both go in," Monty calmly replied. "You get its attention, and I'll get its jaw shut and rewired."

"Sounds like a plan that really shouldn't involve me," I said.

Monty slowly slipped into the pool. "Let's go, Rickey."

The wire was still on the gator, but loose. Stupidly, I followed Monty into the pool, got the alligator's attention, which wasn't hard. Miraculously, and before I passed out, Monty got the gator under control. I don't know if the film sequence made it into the show, but

One of Monty's tigers.

it landed on my resume because Lamont called me again for a roller derby sequence involving a 10-foot alligator—but that's another story.

Eddie Braun hired me to do a big pipe ramp, which as far as I know is the biggest pipe ramp in music video history. He told me it wouldn't be for the faint of heart. I would be wrecking a $60,000 Ferrari at high speed for the Eminem / Dr. Dre music video "I Need a Doctor." Eddie needed a smaller guy like me to fit in the low roof Ferrari and, as he said in the documentary *Gnarly Days*, "There are only a couple of guys I would put in that seat. And frankly, Rick is someone who would go for it."

There wasn't much head room in the car, a stiff roll cage was built so that the roof wouldn't crush my head. Usually, roll cages are built with room between the body and the cage, so it softens the roll-over by the metal giving. I didn't have that choice.

On the day of the shoot, we lost the location in the Santa Monica mountains and had to pick a new one quickly. Between Eddie, Jack, and myself, there was a lot of experience to choose one.

Unfortunately, the only alternate location available was a length of road shaped in an 'S' that had a drop off down an adjacent canyon. We all surmised that if I hit the ramp hot, about 55 plus mph, I would jump over the middle part where the canyon drop off was and start the crash and rolling over on the opposite side of the 'S.'

My safety stuntmen were my sons Mikey and Brian. A helicopter was brought in at the last second to cover the treacherous terrain.

As I was getting dressed in my racing suit, a white Rolls Royce pulled up, and a large, muscular African American man and his beautiful lady stepped from the car and walked toward me. When they got to the director, Allen Hughes (*Book of Eli* and *Menace II Society*), who was standing near me, I was introduced to this large, muscular man.

Eddie and Allen said to him, "This is your stunt double."

We shook hands and exchanged pleasantries, and then he walked away. I thought I was doubling Eminem. Mikey indicated the large gentleman walking away. "Do you know who that is, Dad?"

"No."

"That's Dr. Dre, the biggest rapper in the world."

I turned to Eddie and said, "I'm doubling him?"

I did the rollover, which can be seen on YouTube at the beginning of the music video "I Need a Doctor," along with a second video of Dr. Dre watching my stunt, and then turning to the camera and saying, "Oh, shit!"

With Dr. Dre.

Chuck Norris, me, and Louis Gossett, Jr. on location for *Firewalker*.

Chapter 9:

Memories, Friends, and 8 X 10s

T here is a saying among veteran stunt people that at the end of a stunt person's career, all they have are memories, friends, and 8 X 10s. After working in stunts for more than 35 years, I completely agree with this observation. While I've made a good living doing stunt work and traveled the world and learned a great deal about people, the true payoff has been the extraordinary friendships I've made, all of which are some of my greatest treasures, along with the boxes of photographs spanning over more than three decades. In this chapter, I'd like to share some of these highlights.

Director John Landis began his career in the mail room of 20th Century Fox. A high school dropout, 18-year-old Landis made his way to Yugoslavia to work as a production assistant on *Kelly's Heroes* (1970). Remaining in Europe, he found work as an actor, extra, and stuntman in many of the Italian "spaghetti" westerns. The trademark trivia often mentioned in Landis-directed films is the inclusion in some form of the phrase "See you next Wednesday," which is a reference to a script Landis wrote when he was 15 years old. In the 1980 comedy classic film *The Blues Brothers*, the phrase appears on a billboard where cops are sitting in their cars lying in wait. His son Max is now an accomplished producer and writer.

Legendary stuntman Eddie "The Doughnut" Donno did the phenomenal stair fall in *The Blues Brothers* in which he tumbled end-over-end down a steep staircase while sitting inside a grade school-type desk in which the chair and desk are one unit.

The stair fall was one hell of a stunt that almost killed him, at least in the broad sense of the phrase. As the story goes, moments later, Landis walked over to Eddie, lying there in a daze, and said, "That was great, Eddie. Can you do another one?"

Eddie looked around, appearing confused, and then the focus suddenly returned to his eyes, as he responded immediately, "Go fuck yourself!" It took several minutes for the laughter to die down. Even Landis ended up laughing, which wasn't like him. Landis says it's one of the greatest stunts in history.

Eddie often did things like this on the spur of the moment that were utterly hilarious. We were doing a car jump in Durham, North Carolina. Eddie was driving, and I was the passenger. The director said, "Action" and as the car took off, I felt something fall into my lap. I looked down and found myself staring at Eddie's false teeth, both uppers and lowers. I said, "Oh, my God, what the fuck!" !"

Eddie kept accelerating as we fast-approached the jump ramp. "Don't forget to remind me to put them back in when we cut!" It seemed that he often forgot.

As the car accelerated, he glanced over at me and gummed, "Squeeze your legs together and hold onto 'em!" Apparently, he was tired of having his teeth come out during a horrendous car crash, so, when possible, he entrusted them to whomever he was with.

Eddie was famous for making money in a bar. He was short, but stocky. He'd win all kinds of loot by jumping up onto the bar from a

Rick and Eddie
car jump.

flat-footed standing position on the floor. He was a classic, charismatic, loving, and talented friend.

Colorful, unpredictable stunt people sometimes came in groups. I played in a successful cover band called "Bandit" for a couple years. We often played three times a week—Friday night, Saturday night, and then at a Sunday afternoon motorcycle rally. We played the Londoner in Valencia and the Tree House in Simi and had a loyal following at Doc's in Newhall. Our talented lead singer was a second generation stuntman Brad Orrison. I played saxophone, some lead and backup singing, and percussions.

The Epper family is a legendary stunt family going back to Grandpa Epper, who doubled for the incomparable Gary Cooper, who went by the nicknames "Coop," "Cowboy Cooper," "The Montana Mule," and "Studs."

Some members of the Epper family included Jeannie, Stephanie, Richard, Gary, Eurlyne, Andy, and Tony. One evening, the Eppers

The Band.

came to the Londoner and got a table to celebrate Andy's birthday and drank all night.

Around one in the morning, Brad was feeling no pain and could hardly stand. Ultimately, he fell back into the drums, but we kept playing, and he kept singing. As we started into our next song, I suddenly heard a tremendous commotion. When I looked to where the noise was coming from, I saw the entire Epper family engaged in a stunt fight that looked to be right out of the movie *Hooper*. Chairs flew through the air, fists were flying, tables were upturned—but it was a clean, old-fashioned western barroom brawl among themselves. Eventually, even some of the local patrons got involved.

Grabbing my instrument, I backed off the stage, choking down laughter. When the dust finally settled, the Eppers apologized to all the patrons. Richard Epper then turned to the owner and said, "Don't worry about anything. No need to call the cops. We'll pay for whatever damage we did."

The owner smiled and said, "You don't have to pay for a thing. This is the best night I've ever had in my bar. The bar tab alone, I've never seen anything like this before." He then turned to our band and added, "I'm building a stage for you guys and giving you a one year contract."

When I first got in with stuntmen, many of them were just plain rowdy because they were originally cowboys. Mario Roberts and I got into fun fights when we were Alan Gibbs' fight guys. One day we walked into the lobby of a major hotel in New York and decided to do a picture fight. We beat the crap out of each other and topped it off

BANDIT

HARD ROCK 'N' ROLL BAND

What do harley riders and stuntmen do on the weekends????
They're at your local saloon, bar and pubs
As
BANDIT
On

Saturday December 7th
The
Londoner

18511 Soledad Canyon Road
Canyon Country
(n.w. corner of Sierra Highway and Soledad Canyon Road)
Yes, In the Shopping Center

BRAD ORRISON-GUITAR	PERFORMING:	RICK AVERY-SAX
MICK NELSON-GUITAR	ZZ-TOP	STEVE HOBBS-BASS
DAN HERNANDEZ-DRUMS	LYNYRD SKYNYRD	
	ROLLING STONES	
	BOB SEGER	
	ERIC CLAPTON	
	JIMI HENDRIX	
	And many others	

Bandit "two gun" t-shirts available
Call 661-255-0770 steve
661-795-7708 brad
email: hurrican52@yahoo.com

Hi
Rick —
Practice
falling!
Best
Don
Rickles

Don Rickles.

Above, Alan Arkin, below, me with Henry Winkler.

with Mario dragging me into the elevator and quickly disappearing. Hours later, we returned to the hotel lobby to find cops looking for the two guys, one of whom, the cops surmised, may have committed murder and/or kidnapping. Our picture fights were that convincing.

Doug Coleman, who was a big time stunt coordinator for many years, called one day in 2003 and asked if I'd like to double Dustin Hoffman in the uproarious romance comedy *Meet the Fockers*.

I thought, *Is he serious? I'd double Dustin for free just to say I*

Doubling Dustin.

worked with him. For years, Hoffman had become famous for taking a wide range of difficult rolls, such as a crippled street hustler in *Midnight Cowboy* (1969); an actor pretending to be a woman in *Tootsie* (1982) and an autistic in *Rain Man* (1988).

Ironically, Dustin had attended Santa Monica City College, but dropped out after a year for poor grades. But before he did, he took an interest in acting because he was told that "nobody flunks acting."

When I arrived at the set on the first day, I was a veteran, having worked as a stunt coordinator and second unit director and done hundreds of stunts. I presented myself as a professional who knew what he was doing.

The first scene that required me to double Dustin was simple and involved Dustin doing a dance at a party, and then falling backwards over a table. A choreographer showed me how to moon walk because Dustin was going to be doing the moon walk just before he went over the table.

I was working on the moon walk when Dustin came over to me. After introducing himself, he said, "Rick, I don't want you to do it as good as that. I'm not going to do a great moon walk." He then tied doing the moon walk with his role as a woman in *Tootsie*. "It's kind of like walking in high heels. You know what the trick is to walking in high heels, Rick?"

"No," I replied, wondering how many guys had given Dustin an answer to that one.

"You just think about walking on your toes, and then it's simple." He offered that boyish smile of his, gave me a thumb's up on my moon walk, and departed.

The set was a real bar the size of an average, large living room and it was full of extras attending a party. My job in the scene was to do the moon walk, and then back into a table at butt level and fly backwards over the table. Dustin wanted me to grab the tablecloth on the way down, dragging everything on the table with me.

I said, "No problem. It's just run backwards doing a sloppy moon walk, then sail over the table, taking the tablecloth with me." In the next shot, Dustin, hidden in the tablecloth, would jump up from behind the table and then magically reveal himself with "Ta-da!"

The camera was six feet in front of me when I started, and the set was dead quiet. When Jay Roach said "Action," I did the moon walk running backwards, knowing I was going to hit that table hard. What I didn't want to do was lift up, which would make it look like I knew the table was there, and throw myself over it. When I arrived at the table, I hit the edge hard enough to break my tailbone—and nothing happened. I didn't go over the table because it was right at the level that when I hit it, it stopped me cold. In the ensuing seconds, all that happened was one breakaway glass fell off the table and broke on the floor.

The set fell dead quiet, and all anyone could hear was a single voice that was instantly recognizable as Dustin Hoffman who said, "Well, fuck, I could have done that." The entire crew burst into up-roariously laughter.

The stunt coordinator, Doug Coleman, came to me. His face was pale and there was a concerned look in his eyes. "I know what hap-pened," I said quickly, hoping to appease his nerves. "Don't worry. I've got this. Everything's cool."

The table was redressed and everyone took their places. I looked at the setup again and asked, "Is there any way we can fix the table so I can get a little push off here?" which I should have done in the first place.

"Sure," Jay said. "You can push off a little bit—yeah, we've got multiple cameras. It's fine."

I saw Doug sitting on an apple box that was right under the cam-era that's aimed at me, and I saw his leg nervously bouncing up and down. I looked at him and moved my lips "it's going to be okay" be-cause I knew as a stunt coordinator he was about to become, based on my next performance, either the hero or the zero. Actually, he was already a zero because somebody on the set probably already com-mented to Doug, "Your guy can't go over a table?"

The second take went perfectly; it was all great. Later on in the movie, Doug and I were sitting on the steps to our dressing room as Dustin, who was walking by, said, "Hey, guys, have you ever had a cappuccino?"

"No, never have," I replied.

"You guys come with me, I'm going to show you the right way to make the perfect cappuccino." We walked into his motorhome where I smiled and said hello to Dustin's hairdresser Nina Paskowitz. "I want you guys to sit down on the couch," Dustin continued, "because I'm going to show you how you get the right amount of froth and exact touch of cinnamon. By the way, the name cappuccino comes from the Capuchin friars, referring to the color of their habits. Most people don't know that, but now you do."

To put this in perspective of my being an average citizen, Dustin Hoffman — multiple-Academy Award winning Dustin Hoffman — had just walked by where Doug Coleman and I were sitting and was now making a cappuccino for us and saying, "I want you to think of this place like a boat and we're on the ocean. Anything you want on this boat is yours," and he proceeded to make us a perfect cappuccino.

A few nights later, Joni and I attended the cast and crew screening of *Meet the Fockers*. Moments after everyone was seated, I went out to the lobby to get a bag of popcorn and ran into Dustin. I said "Dustin, what are you doing here?" because he'd already been to the premiere. "We're second rate, we're cast and crew."

Dustin smiled and held up his hand. "I just wanted to come and sit in the back and see everybody's reactions. But Rick, this is all about you. This is your night. So enjoy your evening. I'll be in the back."

That's the kind of man Dustin is. He's a fantastic, down to earth guy. There are a couple of stories about him that always make me laugh when I think of them.

Dustin played Tiny Tim in a middle school production. On a bet, he changed the ending line from "God bless everyone!" to "God bless everyone, goddammit!" on opening night and was subsequently suspended.

During the filming of *Wag the Dog* (1997), Dustin, his co-star Robert De Niro, and director Barry Levinson had an impromptu meeting with then-President Bill Clinton at a Washington hotel. "So what's this movie about?" Clinton asked De Niro. De Niro looked over to Levinson, hoping he would answer the question. Levinson, in turn, looked over to Hoffman, who, realizing there was no one else to pass the buck to, is quoted as saying, "So I just started to tap dance. I can't even remember what I said."

In 1995, Bob Minor called me to come work on a John Singleton film entitled *Higher Learning*. I was hired with another stuntman to be security guards, who break up a fight between actors Omar Epps and Michael Rappaport. Prior to shooting, Bob called me to the set and said, "Check this out, Rick."

Omar Epps and Michael Rappaport were "method" actors. Wanting to get into character, they had been wrestling on the floor for several minutes. This wrestling had nothing to do with the fight that Bob had choreographed, which had Rappaport getting punched in the solar plexus by Omar—which was the cue for me and the other stuntman to intervene and break up the fight.

On take one, the fight was going great when John yelled, "Cut!" Apparently, the fight continued beyond where the punch to the solar plexus took place. John approached the two actors and addressed Michael. "You're supposed to bend over in pain when Omar punches you in the solar plexus. You didn't."

Michael responded, "My character is beyond pain. He doesn't feel it."

John got closer to Michael and punched him with a short one to the solar plexus. Michael doubled over in pain and, gasping for air, heard John utter as he was walking away, "See if your character can get past that pain." OMG, we all had to stifle our laughter.

On take two, Omar and Michael again went past the same spot. John yelled, "Cut!" and yelled up to Michael, "Do you want me to come back up there and show you about pain?"

Michael sheepishly nodded no, and take three was great. John Singleton became my method hero that day.

In 1987, I was working for Alan Gibbs on a film called *Ironweed*, starring Jack Nicholson and Meryl Streep. Jack would work hard every day to prepare with what was scheduled to be shot. Director Hector Babenco made the mistake of changing the order one day, which didn't sit well with Jack.

Jack, the consummate professional, however, prepared for the changed scene and nailed it. Hector said to Jack, as many directors say to their actors and stunt persons, "That was perfect. Let's do one more," to which Jack responded, "If it was perfect, print two," as he left the set and walked back to his trailer.

Every stunt person has their hopefully short list of most embarrassing moments, and I certainly have mine. I was working on a movie called *Get Smart* (2008) starring Anne Hathaway, The Rock, and Steve Carell. Stunt coordinator Doug Coleman called and said he had a big driving sequence for me to do. He wanted me to drive an SUV that was on fire inside and, after a huge car jump, ends up driving along a set of railroad tracks.

The flames inside the SUV were a controlled fire using propane

The flying SUV on fire.

Above, in a scene with Sean Penn; below, with Sylvester Stallone on *Grudge Match*.

With Kevin Hart.

tanks. I wore a helmet and fire retardant Nomex racing suit to protect myself. I asked for, but never received, a mic inside my helmet to communicate with the crew. Earlier, I'd done a Cadillac chase, eventually jumping the car through a shack. The SUV jump was more complicated, so I went to my close friend Craig Hunter to help prep the SUV and build the proper ramp.

Whenever I did a ramp jump or pipe ramp in the past, I would go on instinct and was always on the money. This one was more complicated because Peter Segal, the director, wanted to see the SUV, its interior on fire, jump over a wall on the highway, land 17 feet below, smash into some railway containers, and then end up on a set of railroad tracks.

Jump formula and Lev Yevstratov.

Craig Hunter, who is a master car rigger and talented stunt driver, called Lev Yevstratov, a Russian Physicist who built the innovative Russian Arm, which is a crane affixed to the top of a Mercedes SUV. This Russian Arm has revolutionized the shooting of car commercials and car chases worldwide. Lev is 6'3" and 300 lbs. of big man and laughingly said that calculating the jump and landing amounted to a simple middle school physics problem.

Craig built the ramp and gave me a specific speed of 46 mph to hit it at. This would put the SUV 63 feet from the ramp that would allow enough room for me to land the car and make the turn.

The jump went perfectly with the SUV landing, sideswiping the railroad containers, and then continuing down the tracks. The shot couldn't have gone better, and the SUV was then fitted with special tires that locked its wheels onto the railroad tracks. At this point, I could do no wrong, as everyone on the crew thought I was a fantastic driver.

Over the next few days, I continued driving down the tracks, as we filmed coverage of Ann Hathaway and The Rock doing their coverage in the back. Then on the final day, the last shot had a camera set in the middle of the tracks on a telephoto lens that was affixed to a heavy wooden tripod and aimed directly at the oncoming SUV. Of all the shots in this sequence, this one was the simplest.

The SUV I'd been driving was replaced with a second one to match that part in the script. I asked the director of photography, Oscar winner Dean Semler (I've done four movies with him) how far away I needed to stop. He said, "Nowhere close to camera, Rick. You can stop 50 yards away."

I got in the SUV, lit the fire inside, and on "action" started full speed down the tracks. When I heard "Cut" about 50 yards in, I stepped on the brakes, but the SUV was only marginally slowing down and not coming to a stop. All I had was a portable radio and no mic inside my helmet. The horn was inoperable because we took it

Left, with Dean Semler, D.P. on *Get Smart*, and below, fire inside SUV, My POV.

out with the air bag so they wouldn't go off during a stunt. As a result, I had no way to warn the crew that the SUV might not stop before getting to the $200,000 Panavision Gold camera perched atop the wooden tripod.

As the SUV continued to slow, but on its own terms, I waved

my arms and shouted to the camera crew, who thought that Rick Avery was one of the best drivers in Hollywood, based on the driving they'd witnessed over the past few days. They casually watched as I continued slowing toward them . . . slowing at about 100 feet away to 10 miles per hour . . . then 5 miles an hour . . . I started to believe the car might stop in time, as I wildly waved my arms to warn them, screaming obscenities into my helmet.

As I got within 10 feet of the camera, going less than one mph. I saw the camera crew smiling at me, waiting for me to stop. At five feet, they went from smiles to concerned looks. I said to myself, "Thank God, it's going to stop . . . Yes! Yes! . . . No! . . . No!"

None of them tried to save the camera, as the SUV, almost like a comedy, came to a complete stop, gently nudging the camera and tripod just enough to cause it to tip over in slow motion and go crashing to the ground. Everyone heard the cracking of the lens glass and camera, and those who hadn't been watching suddenly turned their attention to me. Scotty please beam me out of here. The camera crew looked at me disbelievingly. I read on their faces their disapproval and the *How could you* looks.

I got out of the SUV and told everyone that I tried to warn them that the brakes weren't working. As it turned out, we found that no one had disconnected the second SUV's anti-braking system (ABS), so when those special slick tires were placed on the railroad tracks, the ABS did its job and was pulsating in an attempt to slow the vehicle that the system determined was in a skid.

This happened to me once on a Mercedes commercial. The director wanted me to come speeding straight by camera, slam on my brakes, and stop right next to it. No problem. I can hit a mark. I came in hot as I could. It was just a straight stop. I stepped on the brakes and nothing happened. I went sailing by camera and my mark by about 25 yards.

Thankfully, in the Hollywood film business, a person can go

home a zero on Friday, and then go home a hero on the following Monday. Such was the case the day that Cory Eubanks did a BMW commercial in San Pedro.

Cory is the most renowned car guy in the business. He was called upon do to a jump driving a prototype BMW that was followed by a 360-degree slide that was to stop abruptly at the end of a bridge drop off. This was for a BMW spot directed by John Woo. Cory said, "Rick, what do you think will happen if I don't make this mark?"

"You're going to die, dude, are you serious? You'd have a fifty-foot drop in a convertible. You're going to die."

My job was to be a stab car, which had me positioned four blocks down the road behind the wheel of a big station wagon. In the event that Cory's car was out of control after the car landed from the big downhill jump, I'd stab Cory's car with mine, essentially crashing into him to stop him before the BMW destroyed life, limb, and/or property. To increase the safety factor, a second stab car was positioned across from me.

Just below, two guys were manning a camera. Earlier, Cory had expressed to them his concerns about their position and suggested they move the camera. They didn't want to hear it.

"Hey, we've been doing this forever! You do your job and we'll do ours!"

"Fine. Maybe you should at least take the camera's focus puller and put him on the other side rather than . . ."

"We get it!" they insisted.

Cory's car took off. Moment later, he hit the ramp, and when he landed, I saw the car tweak, which suggested to me that something may have broken in the front end, which wasn't unexpected. It appeared as if Cory's car had lost its steering and was now out of control. These thought processes went to minutiae because this was a BMW prototype car worth over a million dollars—and far more importantly,

Cory's life could be in danger. I needed to quickly decide if the prototype going to stop on its own in the street.

I wasn't going to take any chances, even if I ended up totaling the million dollar baby. Cory was all that mattered. I stomped on the gas and came in hot. Lucky for me, I hit Cory's car dead center of its left front wheel, lightly enough to perfectly knock his car away from a surefire crash into the camera crew or homes along the street. What a lucky shot. I don't think I could do it again that perfectly.

When the BMW finally came to a stop. All was quiet and I wasn't sure if I'd made the right decision. Seconds went by that felt like minutes. I was about to become a hero or a zero. Much to my relief, I finally heard the stunt coordinator Greg Smrz say over the radio, "Good job, Rick!"

I then saw Cory get out of his car. He was a half-block down the street from me because he was coming down that hill at a good clip when I hit him. He was walking toward me and the camera with a look of rage. Initially, I thought maybe he was mad at me for doing what I did and damaging the prototype.

He walked toward me and stood next to the two camera personnel and gave them something he picked up in the street. That's how close it came to camera. Moments later, he walked over to me. I said, "What was that?"

"The eyepiece," he said. His car had come so close to that camera that it also sheared of the camera's eyepiece.

"Rick, when I realized I'd lost my steering, I thought for sure I was going to kill those two cameramen. All of a sudden, I felt an angel come and hit my car and nudge it off just enough so that I wouldn't." He then smiled and patted me on the back and said, "Thanks, Buddy."

With LL Cool J.

With Will Farrell.

Chapter 10:

Mission from God

I was convinced that several key films that I worked on as a stunt-man would launch my career. Director John Landis decided to do *Blues Brothers 2000*. In the sequel, Elwood must reunite the old band and, with a few new members, go on another "Mission from God." The movie was shot in Canada because it was cheaper to film there. I was hired on as stunt coordinator and brought six stunt drivers to Canada with me. Half the stunt people were from Canada, and the other half (our core)—Eddie Braun, Hubie Kerns, Jack Gill, Bob Minor, Joni, and myself—were from the United States. Although Alan Gibbs had warned me that my marriage to Joni would be destroyed if she became a stuntwoman, I ultimately helped her get her SAG card, and she went on to have a lucrative career in stunt work.

John Landis loved stuntmen because he loved action. He said in the first production meeting that the Blues mobile in the first movie did a 180-degree slide and parked on the other side of the street be-

Above US stunt drivers, top left to right: Hubie Kerns, Buck MacDancer, Eddie Braun, Jack Gill, Joni, and myself. Kneeling is our special effects person. Left, clowning with director John Landis.

tween two parked cars. "So, Rick, I'd like to redo that again in the second movie. How're you going to do it?"

I gave John a simple answer. "Well, I'm just going to have a good driver come in and he'll throw a 180 and he'll end up on the other curb."

"You're scaring me."

"Why?"

"Because on the first *Blues Brothers*, Eddie Donno drove that car, and they had a box with a special lever or some kind of special thing."

"I'm not aware of any of that," I replied "I'm just going to do it with a driver. I'm going to use Jack Gill." Jack was one of the finest drivers in Hollywood. He was a regular on *Dukes of Hazard* and *Knight Rider* and was fabulous behind a wheel.

Meanwhile the computer graphics imaging (CGI) guy, who was sitting earshot, weighed in. "John, I can put a Maserati and a Ferrari there and make it look like—"

"No, we'll put real cars there." John didn't like computerized stunts. He wanted things practical.

The night of the shooting, the street on which Jack Gill had to drive the car was wet. The visual was that the car was driving in one direction, then made a screeching 180-degree turn, and as it did, slid sideways into a tight parking place at the curb on the opposite side of the street between two cars. I went to John and asked how much distance he wanted between the bumpers of the cars? John said he wanted three feet.

Oh my god, three feet on the first take? I was nervous and certain I was going to be on a plane. Jack wasn't too happy and a little nervous, as well. John was a tough director and often began each gag by telling the stunt people, "Don't fuck this up."

There was pressure on Jack, no doubt. I told the teamsters who were positioning the two cars between which Jack had to slide the Blues mobile, "Back them up a little bit. John will never know," which was what Alan Gibbs used to say about Hal Needham. Hal would say, "I want you coming around this corner at 100 miles an hour," and Alan would say, "Come around 40, he won't know the difference." So I was taking on the same philosophy—four feet, John won't know the difference. What I didn't know was that John was standing behind me when I said that.

"Get a grip over here and get me a tape measure," he growled. "I want this measured three feet."

Jack came in on the first take and nailed it perfectly, did a 180-degree sliding turn and put the car dead center between the two cars parked at the curb. No one could have done it better. John Landis said, "Cut! Okay, we're going to do it again" and told the teamsters to move the cars in a foot each. So now there was a two-foot margin for the front and rear ends of the Blues mobile. Jack nailed it on the second take.

Now it was a game to John, or a challenge. What were we going to do? Wreck a couple of cars? He said make it a foot. So Jack backed up the car to his start point, waited for "Action!" and then did the gag again and nailed it. It was amazing to watch. After saying, "Cut," John Landis merely shook his head and walked off. Sometimes a person has to be satisfied with their own results.

The original *Blues Brothers* film had a breathtaking entrance of the flaming Blues Mobile dropping from a height of 80 feet at the Blues Brothers' "comeback gig." John Landis walked into my office during pre-production and said, "You know, I'm realizing, Rick, we had a lot of action—actually we destroyed an entire mall—in *The Blues Brothers*. This picture doesn't have that kind of action. I need to beef something up. Why don't you put together something at the end where we have five cars pile up."

"Sure. That's great. We'll turn over a car. Great fun." Back then, just one car rollover in a movie was a big thing.

On a film shoot when there's a bunch of stunt guys getting ready to do a car chase, the stunt coordinator gets down on the sidewalk, draws lanes with chalk, and brings out his toy Hot Wheels. Then he'll say, "Rick, you're the red car; Cory, you're the blue car; Don, you're the black car" and then tells each stunt person their specific job.

I went to the toy store and bought five miniature Hot Wheels cars and figured out my setup in five minutes. Every few days, however,

John would stick his head in the door and up the ante. "Make that ten cars," then a day later, "Make that fifteen." My eyes were widening. This was fantastic. Was he serious? A 15-car pileup? A week later, he increased the number to 25 cars, then 30, then—"You know what? Let's try forty cars." Oh my God, and he wants turnovers and multi-car crashes. And all he said was "Design it."

I asked, "Can you give me the basic idea?"

"Well, they're going to run into one of those huge cement pavers that pour highway lanes. The Blues mobile comes up and it's being chased by fifty police cars." The Blues mobile had the capability of jumping a 200-foot jump, which is two-thirds of a football field. "The Blues mobile will jump over the paver, and the other cars won't."

Pipe ramps.

"How do you want it to end up, John?"

"I want it to end up in one huge pile of cars."

"You got it. How much time do we have to do this?"

"Two days."

Typically, in Hollywood back then, to shoot a single car rollover would take a half day because a pipe ramp, which is what the car launches off, needed to be set up, as well as the camera crews and rehearsals. That would be for only one rollover, and John wanted a 54-car pileup in two days. In order to accomplish this, I developed a way that all the cars stayed within a specific area and actually end up in one enormous heap.

I had plenty of cars. Weeks earlier, I purchased several dozen Canadian police cars and had them painted and then stripped inside except for a driver's racing seat. To prepare for this stunt, I brought up Bill Jenkins from Los Angeles to show the local effects guy how to build a roll cage. We had to build 54 roll cages in as many police cars.

Because I wanted every car to be exactly alike, we tested all 54 cars and made notes as to which cars needed tune-ups, which needed tires, brakes, and emergency brakes. I had roll cages and racing seats

put in every car and purchased 54 pair of 5-point harnesses and lightweight Kevlar helmets with a special neck brace for each driver.

The Blues Mobile used on *Blues Brothers 2000* was a former police car fitted with a 400-horsepower NASCAR stock engine and a nitro button capable of boosting the car's horsepower to 700 in order to accommodate assorted automotive mayhem. I had 18 Blues mobiles built for this movie, four of which ran on nitrous. We had crash cars, jump cars, extra handling cars—18 altogether. For good reason, the Blues Mobile was acknowledged by all as a magical vehicle that could, among other things, fly, park anywhere it wanted, and drive underwater.

I showed up the day we started testing all of the police cars and saw one of them doing 90 degree slides, reverse 180s, and slides up to a wall. What I found odd was that I didn't see a driver, only a passenger in the front seat. On closer inspection, I saw a little blond head just above the steering wheel. Then I suddenly realized—OMG it was Mikey! Eddie Braun was sitting in the right seat showing Mikey how to slide a car. Eddie was notorious for doing this kind of stuff.

But I was the stunt coordinator and had to show some maturity in case anything bad happened so I screamed "EDDIE!" They stopped immediately. I was proud and pissed at the same time. That day was a good memory for Mikey, though.

The multi-car pileup was a challenge. I got five Hot Wheels cars on a table in my office and talked it out to myself, "Okay, this is how he's going to crash. I'm going to have this guy T-bone, he's going to run in at 30 miles per hour and cram himself into that cement spreader. Then I'll have the next five cars slam into the back of him—which will serve as the base of the incoming pileup and hide the ramps for the next run of cars."

I had the first five cars come in, and then I said, "That's five, that's ten, and then I'll have this guy come in and we'll have small jump ramps set up. Then I'm going to have the guys come up the back of those cars and they'll do little short jumps and they'll land on top of those cars and that'll build the pile a little bigger."

When I got up to ten cars, I started to invent things. After I had the initial jump ramps in place, I had bigger jump ramps, and the

new wave of drivers would start coming in. I built pipe ramps, but I had to build three pipe ramps in the street, and I had drivers do right-wheel-down, left-wheel-down, and one guy center-punch. Then I had two guys drive up the same pipe ramp, one right after the other. It finally came down to the last two days of filming. We were well prepared with talent and equipment.

The first day we did a 10-car pile-up, and it was hellacious, but John didn't think it was fast enough. So on the next take, he said he wanted to re-do that original car wreck and made it clear that he didn't want to use the guys who did the crashes on the previous take. He wasn't pleased with it, and that's the way John was.

I asked for volunteers from my group of Canadians and Americans. I wanted to use mostly Canadians in this first car crash. A little guy in back raised his hand, and said, "I'll do it."

I replied, "You've got to come in fast and hit this cement spreader really hard."

"I will, Mr. Avery. I can do it."

Ten cameras rolled speed for take two, and this time the stunt drivers came in hot. When the little guy came in, his car's windshield and front console broke loose and ended up bruising his chest. Even though we had Lexan (a thin, clear polycarbonate protective sheet) affixed to the windshield, he hit so hard that his car's rear end came up, and the second car crashed under the first car's undercarriage. Had the windshield gone another four inches, it could have killed him. I ran over after the take to check on him. The paramedics had gotten to him first.

"Is he okay?" I asked anxiously.

"He's fine. He just has a bruise."

Just then, I spotted some kind of device attached to his chest.

"What's that?"

One of the paramedics answered, "It's a pacemaker."

"What?" I looked in shock at the Canadian stunt driver. "You're wearing a pacemaker? You didn't tell me you have a heart problem and you're doing this?"

The guy looked back at me apologetically and said, "Would you let me do it if I told you?"

"No, I wouldn't have, but you did a great job." The guy left the set that day a hero. He lived my mantra—a life at risk. Sadly, we lost him a few years later to a heart attack. I find solace in knowing he was able to achieve his dream.

After we did the first 10 car crashes, we started our car jumps and we did 10 or 15 of those. Then we went on to the car rollovers. First they were at lower speeds, 30 to 40 mph, until we got to the last ones, which needed to come in at speeds closer to 60 mph in order to land higher up in the pile.

The stunt drivers who worked on this film knew what it took to do a huge jump or car rollover. In the United States on previous motion pictures, stunt drivers did one car rollover on a movie, and then they may not get another rollover for a year or two, or even five years—or maybe they'd never get one.

In this case, most of the drivers did up to five rollovers in one day. Since they knew they would be paid big bucks per rollover, they said, "Rick, don't take me out of sequence. Pour me into the next car if you have to because I just want to keep doing them."

After performing a number of rollovers, several drivers got loopy because they were semi-concussed. Joni did four or five jumps and rollovers. On the first jump, she center-punched it and landed on Buck McDancer's car. It was a triple turnover with three cars involved and she injured her back. We didn't know she hurt her back because she went on to do several more turnovers until the pain was too severe for her to continue.

Hubie Kerns came to me after he'd done four or five rollovers and said, "Rick look at the sky, it's just so beautiful." I figured he was high as a kite from a mild concussion, so I retired him for the day. Eddie Braun talked about his eyes almost popping out. He'd already done a car jump of 200 feet, plus four car rollovers, and he couldn't do anymore, so I had to pull him.

What I told these drivers was, "As soon as you get done with your

pipe ramp, get out of the car, and if you can walk, go back and hop into another car." Then when everyone, including camera, was set for the next wave, I'd say, "Action!" and we did it again.

These guys would be running back and forth, adrenalin flowing, making bucks and movie history. We found out that the limit that anyone could do was five, because after that, the person was whacky.

Because we ran five cars at a time, I had five paramedic ambulances standing by. Figuring the worst case scenario if all five drivers got knocked out, I wanted a paramedic team for each driver. In addition,

I had forklifts that could quickly move cars if a driver got trapped. We also had stunt safety teams assigned to every driver and car to harness them in and get them out after the driver gave a thumb's up.

We did no more than five cars at one take and no rehearsals. After five drivers would crash their cars, we'd cut, which would allow them to get out of the cars. If we saw a vacated car where a driver was in line with what the viewer would see, we put a dummy behind the wheel.

Even the best laid plans can have dire mishaps. Bob Minor, a veteran stuntman of massive stature and physique, did a small turn-over and was knocked out cold. The problem was his car came to rest upside down. This was exactly why I had those forklifts there, because if a driver was upside down, I wanted that car made upright so that the paramedics could get to him. I got two thumbs up from Joni and Buck's safety teams, but thumbs down from Bob's. My heart stopped. I raced to the side of Jack Gill, who was Bob's safety.

Everyone stood around while Jack Gill was looking at his watch and saying, "It's been two minutes. It's been five minutes. I don't know how many minutes." That was a long time hanging upside down in a harness, and Bob wasn't responding. When I began to see him drooling from his mouth, I feared he was going to die. Finally, the rescue team got him out, and a helicopter transported him to a hospital. After remaining in a coma for two days, he finally made a full recovery.

Because we ran out of qualified drivers, I drove several of the final cars. It was quite a sight to be the fifth car behind four cars speeding to three pipe ramps in front of me. I watched the lead cars getting airborne, spiraling and pirouetting against the blue sky, as I launched following the pandemonium. It was a spectacular view, and one that I don't think any other stuntman has ever seen. I felt privileged to see that as I raced to the ramp at 55-plus mph as the last car.

I have an Internet radio show called Hardknocks that features interviews with extreme athletes from many popular sports. I hosted the show with my sons Mikey and Brian. We did 73 episodes that can be

Recording Hardknocks TV.

downloaded from iTunes or heard at hardknocks.tv. We had racing legend Mario Andretti and NFL football legend Bill Romanowski, among many others.

One of my favorite questions was to get inside the head of my guest at the precise moment that he was about to perform. One day, for fun, I spoke into a digital recorder, reliving my mental state from just prior to taking off toward the ramp through to the end of the rollover.

Toronto, Canada . . . the biggest car wreck sequence in movie-making history . . . 40 cars in and we've run out of stuntmen. It's my time . . . racing suit on . . . squeeze in the small driver's window through the roll cage . . . stunt safety helps me put on my five-point seat belts . . . cinch 'em down so tight I almost can't breathe . . . put on my collar protection . . . now it's even harder to breathe . . . time for the helmet . . . Everything on . . . can barely move . . . barely reach the steering wheel . . . wrist restraints on to keep my arms from flailing out of the window and getting broken if I get knocked out. Ready. Five cars going at once . . . three in front of me . . . one to my right . . . can't see to the side . . . "Action!" comes over the radio. Been here before dozens of times . . . I'm calm . . . adrenalin back again . . . my friend . . . just keep it in check . . . a little good . . . keep it under control . . . I see three cars in front of me take off for the three pipe ramps . . . I give them a beat and I stomp on the gas . . . gotta get to 55-60 mph . . . Jack Gill on speed gun . . . I see the cars in front hit the ramps and fly into the air like twisting missiles . . . Gonna be me in a second . . .

I'm at the wheel, heading for the top of the pile!.

concentrate . . . put the ramp on the inside of the wheel . . . not too much or you'll center punch it . . . noisy engine running up the ramp . . . then deathly quiet . . . all I see is sky twisting . . . flying thirty feet in air . . . one, two, three . . . then IMPACTS onto the cars already wrecked on the ground . . . holding onto the wheel for dear life . . . thumbs out so I don't break them . . . the car twists, slams, rolls . . . 3,000 pounds of steel around me . . . such unimaginable G-forces on my body . . . it has to be this way to look good . . . the more it tosses, impacting, the happier I am . . . the sorer I will be. Finally, the car comes to rest . . . safety guys come out . . . give a thumb's up so they can tell paramedics and first assistant director I'm ok . . . satisfied . . . hero . . . get out . . . Back to do it all over again in another car on another take . . . I'm happy.

The rapid-fire crash that appeared at the end of the film for less than two minutes took four months to plan and three days to shoot using multi-camera setups. Utilizing the skills of some of the top drivers in the stunt industry, our stunt crew jumped and crashed 54 cars in different directions, at varying heights and speeds, into a cement spreader, a dump truck, a trailer, and each other. It was as if we took all the cars that were crashed throughout the first Blues Brothers movie and crashed them together in this one sequence. I hold the record for the biggest car wreck in the history of cinema. A fact that was submitted to the *Guinness Book of Records* movie version where we crashed 54 cars in three days. It was a great feeling of accomplishment. But no one saw the movie, and because it didn't do well, the sequence went unappreciated.

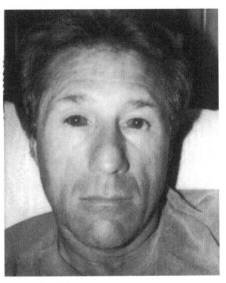
Vampire eyes.

We wrapped that day, and at the wrap party we were stars. When I looked in the mirror the next morning, my eyes were so red from the G-forces that I instilled on myself that I couldn't see the white in my eyes. All I could see was blood red. I looked like a vampire.

The following day when I arrived in the United States and went through customs, I wore sunglasses. The customs agent asked me what I was doing in Canada, and I told him I was a stuntman working on a movie. He said, "You don't look like a stuntman. You don't look broken up or anything. Is that what you do?"

I said, "Yeah," and I raised my glasses and he saw my eyes.

"Ow! Okay, move on. Welcome home."

Filmgoers who see the movie today believe that those crashes were computer generated images (CGI), that there weren't people driving those cars. Even some stunt people don't believe it. But there was a driver behind the wheel of every one of those vehicles.

I was convinced when I got home after this movie that millions of moviegoers would see it and that for the rest of my life, I'd get the call for every motion picture that involved car work. Unfortunately, few people saw the movie that ended up being a flop. It got bad reviews and it wasn't promoted. So I didn't get a lot of hoopla about it. As a matter of fact, I got no hoopla.

There was one enormous plus, however, that made my work on that movie all worthwhile. In the *Blues Brothers 2000* script, the Blues Brothers band was going to compete against "The Louisiana Gator Boys" band in a competition held in New Orleans. The members of the Louisiana Gator Boys weren't actors playing musicians and singers, but instead many of the greatest recording artists spanning over several decades, including Jeffrey "Skunk" Baxter, Gary U.S. Bonds, Eric Clapton, Clarence Clemons, Jack DeJohnette, Bo Diddly, Jon Faddis, Isaac Hayes, Dr. John, Tommy McDonnel, Charlie Musselwhite, Billy Preston, Lou Rawls, Joshua Redman, KoKo Taylor, Travis Tritt, Jimmie Vaughan, Grover Washington Jr., Willie Weeks, and Steve Winwood.

They all showed up, and each and every one of them was personally brought into the production office by John Landis, proclaiming, "You've got to see this!" and then he'd show them raw footage of the Blues mobile's 180-degree skid and parking maneuver.

Given my lengthy music background that included playing sax in a band, when these legendary musicians came out of the production office, I was like a kid in a candy store. I hustled over to them and, trying not to grovel, asked, "Do you mind if I take a picture with you?"

They'd respond, "You want a picture with me? Oh no, I just saw that footage. I want a picture with you!"

With Steve Winwood and Clarence Clemons.

Chapter 11:

The Risk Gene

Psychologists have for years proven that all extreme athletes, including stunt people, have an A-type personality that recently has been further defined as including a "risk gene." To me, this is both a blessing and a curse because this gene allows me to taste life more than most, yet at the same time doesn't prevent me from taking absurd risks.

Who else would say they're looking forward to throwing themselves down a flight of stairs? I don't know where that comes from. I can't wait to throw myself off the side of a building? Wow, I can't wait to do my first fully-engulfed fire burn!?

When I began doing stunts, I brought with me the determination I had to pass my green belt test when I had severely injured my knee. After I'd worked in the movie and television business for a number of years, I began to experience what every stunt person feels—that inner voice that causes them to question whether they'll come home that night.

Cory Eubanks did the bus canon turnover in *Fast and Furious 5*. No one had ever done a cannon turnover of that magnitude in a bus with three cannons going off. In a cannon turnover, a telephone pole or pipe is welded to the underside of the vehicle, then a powder charge fires the pipe to the ground, the result of which hurls the vehicle into the air. Cory told me later that the night before doing the gag that he'd looked at his suitcase and packed all his stuff because he didn't know if he was going to make it back the next day. Essentially, the night before doing that highly dangerous bus turnover, he had gotten all his life's affairs in order, which amounted to that one suitcase.

That's the mindset I tried not to have when I went to work each day as a police officer. There were times when I was in the thick of it and didn't know if I was going to go home, the hospital, or the morgue. In a strange way, that's the allure of police work. I could be driving down the street, and all of a sudden I'm in the midst of a car chase or an armed robbery. I didn't live every day with the mindset of I may not come home tonight, because if I felt that way, I wouldn't have taken the job. But I knew, as with stunt work, that being a policeman came with a fair degree of danger, and I liked walking the edge.

I always knew that what I did was just for a movie, and yet I was willing to jump off a building or roll a car that could have gone over a cliff. Eventually, I recognized that my willingness to take extraordinary risks simply boiled down to one thing—it's my nature.

I learned on the first day I met Kim Kahana at his stunt school that getting into stunt work could sometimes mean risking my life and my heath. I know many stunt people who are on their second hip or knee replacement. Some are totally disabled. Fortunately, I've never had a life-threatening accident, although I've certainly had far more job related injuries than the average Joe. Over the past 35 years, I've had two major ankle sprains, a broken ankle, broken hand, broken finger, broken cheek bone, three knee surgeries, a rotator cuff surgery, a shoulder separation, a broken wrist, and three fused neck vertebrae.

After I'd been doing stunts for three years, Alan Gibbs gave me my first car rollover on the movie *Armed and Dangerous.* He kept asking me for a week, "Are you sure you want to do this?"

"Yeah, sure I want to do it, Alan, of course. I can't wait for this."

The next day, he'd ask again, "You sure you want to do this?"

"Yeah, I'm positive."

He kept asking me, and finally I said, "Stop asking me. Yes, I want to do this. Why do you keep asking me?"

He said "Because I've had to take over for so many stunt guys that said they wanted to do a rollover, and then at the last minute they all of a sudden hurt their back getting into the car, and I had to get in and do it."

"Well, if I hurt my back—or even <u>break</u> my back—you still fit me in the car because I'm going to do it." Was this grit or just plain crazy?

Yeah, I'm positive! My first car rollover.

I didn't know, but it was the way I chose to live this life that I've been blessed with.

In 2000, I worked on an episode of the TV action, crime series *18 Wheels of Justice* that was filmed in San Diego. The show's second unit director, Russell Solberg, an accomplished stuntman and bull rider, called and said, "I'm doing this show in San Diego. Can you do a grab strap?"

"Yeah, how fast do you want it?"

"Forty-five maybe."

"Okay."

A grab strap turnover is where the stunt person grabs onto a strap (often leather or a section of seatbelt) that is bolted to the passenger side floorboard. The driver has no harness or neck brace, just the strap to hold their body down tight to the seat and a lap belt. I did one before for Eddie Braun. He said, "Do you want me to spend money on a roll cage or put that money in your pocket? If I do the roll cage, you'll make two thousand dollars less money."

"Put the whole thing in my pocket of course," I said, smiling.

A grab strap is similar to a rodeo bull rider whose only connection to the bull is the thick leather strap that he affixes to one of his hands. This strap is so vital to the bull rider that he spends considerable time wrapping and pounding on this strap, and not until he's convinced the connection is as strong as he can make it will he signal to turn the bull loose.

When I arrived at the location, I was told that the car I was to drive was to go up a pipe ramp and then down a hillside embankment. I donned my helmet and grabbed onto the looped section of seatbelt that came up from the passenger floorboard.

I cinched up my belt and hit the gas. As I approached the pipe ramp, I checked the speedometer and the lineup. When doing a pipe ramp, the front tire must hit within a five-inch area. The width of a tire has to be at a certain spot and at a certain speed; otherwise the car can get center-punched and won't turnover—or it can miss the pipe ramp entirely and hit the camera and crewmembers. Once the setup and approach is locked in, the driver has to get down because if they sit up and there's no roll bar in the car, the driver can end up—well, a little roughed up. I usually lay down on the seat, lock my right elbow into the grab strap, and then grab my right wrist with my left hand to hold me in.

Grab strap sequence.

As the car went off the embankment and tumbled end-over-end down the hillside, my mind was saying, *why is your left hip up on the roof? No, it's not on the roof, it's in the seat, but why is it on the roof again? What's going on here?* The car finally stopped, ending up on its tires, which was rare. Russell Solberg scurried down the hill and asked, "How was it?" ?"

I knew I wasn't seriously injured, but I was still confused. "I think my left hip is a little sore. I think it hit the roof, but how could that happen?" I looked down and said, "My belt came loose."

"Your belt came loose?"

I had locked down my seatbelt, and right before the director said action, I double-checked my belt and then took off. I couldn't figure out how it came loose until years later a stuntman said it had happened to him. "If you've got your release, it's a little bar pointed to the left. And when you reached over to grab your wrist, the sleeve on your fire suit hit that latch and you unlatched yourself."

So that's what had happened! At least I proved one thing—that a stunt driver can do a multiple turnover without a seatbelt and just a grab strap and their hips will take it. Sort of.

For most stunt people, nothing is more potentially dangerous than a propane mortar that puts out a huge explosion of fire. They're extremely hot and fast and come in small, big, and monster sizes.

Air Force One (1997) starring Harrison Ford had a monster fireball that was hot enough to incinerate anyone it hit. It went off in a helicopter in a scene that required me and several other stuntmen to fall down. I was on top of the roof and asked the special effects guy, "Frazier, how far out is this going to go?"

"Twenty feet maybe," he replied. "As it goes out, it raises up, so if you and the other guys get to your mark, fall down when it goes off and you'll be all right. It'll go right over your heads."

I trusted him because he'd done lots of big movies that involved high explosives. But the scary part was this could be a bad day. The most terrifying part wasn't when the action cue was called and I ran and the explosion went off. It was going back to the number one mark and standing three feet in front of this monstrous mortar. If somebody hit that button prematurely, or even accidentally, I wouldn't know because I'd be gone in a flash. I suppose the feeling is akin to the men who load live bombs onto Air Force bombers or search out live land mines.

Thankfully, the shot went exactly as Frazier had said, but that's an example of *am I going to come home today?* I just came here to do a little sequence. Why am I standing here? My ass is puckered so tight that Hulk Hogan couldn't get a rectal thermometer up there if he used all his might. What got me there was that I'm both blessed and cursed by the risk gene.

In 1991, I did a 30-person ratchet on *Batman Returns*, which was the first of four Batman movies I worked on. Fifteen couples danced on a tempered glass floor. Beneath the floor were mortars that were

Flying Dancers.

set to blow the glass apart. All of us were attached to wires hooked to ratchets that were connected to hydraulic machines. At the exact moment the Penguin came through the floor, the mortars were activated, blowing apart the glass as all 30 dancers wearing masquerade masks were rocketed out of scene by the hydraulics to land on tables, floor, and walls.

When that glass blew, I was simultaneous yanked by a wire. I looked down and the glass followed me. It came up to my knees, seemingly in slow motion—that's how close it was. What occurred to me afterwards was that had those mortars accidentally gone off prematurely, the horrifying result would have been 30 double-amputees.

I've never been a real cowboy. In 1990, I got a call from Monty Cox, who was a good stuntman and known for his work with exotic animals, including the Siegfried and Roy tigers and the Exxon tiger. Monty was doing a TV movie in Montana called *Son of the Morning Star*, which was the story of General Custer and Crazy Horse, and the events prior to and during the Battle of the Little Bighorn. Monty

Monty Cox and me.

Rick far right, can't ride a lick.

called and gave me the specifics and then said, "You can ride a horse, can't you?"

"Sure, I can ride a horse," which was enough to get me the job.

When I arrived at the set, I learned that the boss wrangler was a gruff ole grouch named Rudy Ugland, who did many of the great westerns. Also present were a half-dozen veteran stunt cowboys (the real deal cowboys)—Clifford Happy, the Burtons (David and Billy Jr.), Freddy Hice, Richard and Andy Epper—along with Hal Burton and Tom Elliot and a legendary fall horse named Twister. During the two weeks that we were on location, I was hired to alternate between being an American Indian and a member of General Custer's cavalry, which meant that I often changed wardrobe and horses and shot myself.

In my first shot, Billy Burton, Jr. and I galloped our horses past camera. I was later told that when Rudy saw me, he walked over to

Eddie Donno, who was the stunt coordinator, and said, "What the hell you got Avery on that horse for? He can't ride a lick. He sucks."

I was pissed off because Rudy didn't know shit about me. Granted, I wasn't a slappin' leather cowboy, but I could ride a horse.

The next day, my son Brian, who was 17, visited the set and was sitting next to Monty. We were shooting near where Brian lived with his mother in Billings, Montana. It was a special, cherished time that I could spend with my son, and I was proud to have him there. The director, Mike Robe, was shooting a huge master shot that included saddle falls and rearing horses. My job was to ride up a hill and get shot, then fall off the side of my horse. To my right, Clifford Happy was supposed to rear his horse at the same time.

Mike yelled "Action!" I charged up the hill and got shot off my horse using a "step" that was rigged near my stirrup. Clifford's horse slipped while rearing, and his hooves landed on top of me. The horse tried to get away from me but because it was on a hill, it couldn't. So its 1,800-pound body was doing a dance me. I looked up and saw Clifford yanking on the reins and trying to stop the horse from stomping all over my right hip. Fortunately, I was wearing my "coopers" (hockey hip and thigh pads) under my uniform.

Realizing I couldn't take much more of this, I flipped onto my other side and the horse pounded and crashed down on my other hip. Meanwhile, my son turned to Monty and asked, "Who's that?" because the crew and a group of medics, prepared for the worse, were racing toward me with a stretcher.

Monty, in his nonchalant manner, calmly said, "It's your dad."

As I heard the first assistant director screaming into his bullhorn, "CUT! CUT! CUT!" Clifford managed to get his horse off me, and then kneeled at my side and started apologizing profusely.

"Don't worry, Cliff. This wasn't your fault."

"Are you okay?" he kept asking, almost pleadingly.

To my amazement, I was. Sitting up slowly, I gingerly felt my legs

Rick second from right, "He can ride."

and hips, then stood and hobbled back to where everyone was hanging out with the horses. As my son and others were congratulating me for "going big," Rudy appeared on his horse. He stopped and towered above me because I was sitting down. "You can ride on my shows anytime, Rick. You did a damn good job." I made my bones with him that day, and I was especially proud that he said that in front of my son.

An hour later, we were all riding in a rented yellow school bus, heading back to the hotel. I was feeling my oats, and during the hour drive, I playfully gave the cowboys a ration of crappola. "Oh, you guys call this cowboy stuff hard shit? I'm used to getting hit by a car. I'm used to rolling cars. This falling off horses is pussy stuff. Give me a good flight of stairs anytime! Anyway, speaking of falling, try not to fall over each other when you race to the bar to buy me a drink!"

When an hour later we pulled up in front of the hotel, everyone began bailing from the bus except me. Brian noticed I was still sitting.

"C'mon, Dad, let's go," he said.

"Hold on," I replied, stifling a groan. "Just sit down."

"What's the matter? Everyone's going."

The hour drive had resulted in my body stiffening up, and I was now feeling the effects of the horse's ground and pound. If these cowboys saw me after all the bravado I gave them, they'd be all over me like a cheap hooker. I sent my son out to confirm they were all at the bar, after which he helped me limp stealthily at a snail's pace into the hotel.

The next morning, my body was a road map of bruises. But thanks to a long soak in a hot bath and a few prescription pain pills, I reported to the set and did five more saddle falls because that's what a stuntman does. If those cowboys on that show never knew what really happened, if they read this book, they know it now. Don't call me, boys.

In 1988, I got a call from big time TV director Rod Holcomb, who said, "Rick, I'm at the Grand Bay Hotel in Miami. Can you slide down the face of a building?"

"How high?" I asked.

"Pretty high, Rick. I'm driving by it now right now. I think it would be a cool sequence."

"Send me a picture," I responded.

Alan Gibbs had just died, so I didn't have Alan's expertise to go to. But I had Richard Epper, who was a protégé of Alan's and one of the best riggers in the business. When the photo arrived, Richard and I saw that the face of the Grand Bay Hotel was a 45-degree angle, and 155 feet tall. I told Rod that Richard Epper and I could do it.

Richard and I flew to Miami and went to the top of the building. He put me on a descender, which is a wire coiled on a drum with a brake on it. This descender, which was new to stunt work, allowed a stuntman to come off a building, and instead of doing a high fall onto an airbag, he'd be on a wire. During the editing process, the editor would have to hide that wire, but today it's easily taken out with computer graphics imaging.

We had a week to rehearse, so we got right to it. We climbed to the roof, and Richard let me go on the wire, and after I slid for a while, I got so hot that I had to stop. Richard, who is an old cowboy, said, "Okay, I have an idea. Is there a western store in Miami?"

"Hell, I don't know, pal. Let's go find out. They have to have saddles here."

Within a few hours, we found a saddle maker who sewed together a thick leather vest that I could wear so the slide wouldn't burn my back. In the old days, Richard knew from his dad about these vests that were used for drags. Today, this is old technology. The problem, however, was that it took 50 feet before I started to pick up speed. Silicone spray didn't remedy the problem. Next we got rollers off of vacuum cleaners and fastened them onto my back, which also didn't work.

After a couple of days of scratching our heads raw, I said, "You know what I think we need to do? Do you know that Wile Coyote cartoon where he just all of a sudden, bang, off he goes?"

Richard thought for a moment, then a light went off. "That's it! We'll get 185 feet of bungie so you'll have the descender wire on your neck and you'll have the bungie connected at your groin area."

"Uh-oh," I said.

"And when they say action," Richard continued, "I'll release the bungie that will send you down that hill. I think this will work."

On the day of shooting, Rod called for action and off I went. I was on the wire, and Richard would stop me at 185 feet where the building ended, so that I wouldn't go off the building. In the movie there's a cut, and John Travolta, who I was doubling, falls into a pool. But where I did it, there was a 20-foot space that prevented me from making it to the pool, so I had to stop.

I was cooking. I was burning the clothes off my back every take and getting a thousand dollars each time I did it. I performed that slide 18 times and made $18,000, but I told Richard, "Something is going to go wrong. We're tempting fate and making it look too easy."

Sliding down the Grand Bay Hotel.

It was good money, but Rod kept wanting to do it, and I sensed that something bad was going to happen. I said to Richard, "I'll tell you what. On the next one, brake me a little hard, and I'll act like it hurts me."

On the next run, Richard broke me hard. I didn't have to act. It looked like it broke my back, and the director said, "Okay, we're not doing that again. We've done this enough."

Chapter 12:

Laughter, Tears, and Near-Catastrophes

T
he Hollywood film industry is similar to people who enter politics in that one major mistake can end one's career. Rub a powerful person the wrong way, make a wrong comment at the wrong time, get caught up in a scandal, and it could spell the end. Hollywood, like politics, can often feel like dancing in a minefield.

I made one such horrendous slip of the tongue that nearly ended my longstanding good working relationship with Warner Brothers, which has always been one of the most powerful motion picture studios in Hollywood, if not the world.

I'd already done *Batman Begins* (2005) with director Chris Nolan and Wally Pfister as the director of photography. The movie was filmed in Chicago, which was to be Gotham City. The movie was a huge success, and now Warner Brothers was going to do the sequel *The Dark Knight* (2008), which was also filmed in Chicago.

Joni and I were close friends with Tom Struthers, who was the assistant stunt coordinator. He offered Joni stunt work on the movie, and so she came out with me. Score! A double check!

Joni and I did all the prep, and I wasn't myself. I was treating the production assistants badly and had a lot of attitude. My contract included a rental car that I parked in an area where the dressing rooms were located. I pulled into a small dirt lot and went upstairs to the dressing room. A few minutes later, a teamster, who worked with the film's transportation department, yelled up to me, "Hey, fella, how long you gonna be there?"

"As long as it takes," I snarled with an attitude.

Five minutes later, I returned to my car to find that this teamster and a group of his buddies had blocked the exit. He came over to me and began to chew me out. I said, "Who the fuck do you think you're talking to?" He started to put his hand on my shoulder and I knocked his arm off. "You touch me again, I'll knock you out."

"I'm going to call your boss," the teamster said, hoping to intimidate me.

"Call him!"

Tom Struthers came out and found himself in the middle. He wasn't the main stunt coordinator, but his job was to keep everybody in the crew happy. His job wasn't to have some stuntman causing problems.

My experience when I worked as a coordinator was that if a teamster had a problem with one of my stunt people, I'd chew out the stunt person later, but I'd defend him publicly. Tom told me to leave, which I did because I figured he'd have my back.

For the next two days, people on the set were avoiding me. I finally said to Tom, "What's going on? I'm getting a vibe here."

"Well, mate, it's not good. The teamsters want you out of here now. They want you fired."

"Fired? What? Fuck the teamsters."

"No, it's bigger than that."

"Why is it bigger than that?"

"They went and complained to the director."

"What?!" That was unconscionable. I don't care if I was the worst person in the world. A transportation coordinator doesn't go to the director with a problem with a stuntman. I couldn't believe it.

"Okay, what do I have to do to make this better?" I asked. "You want me to apologize to this guy?" Although Tom had my back, this was the stunt coordinator, Paul Jennings', problem. "Fuck that teamster," I continued. "But I'll apologize to him if it'll help. I'll be the bigger man."

This became a three-hour issue one night, and the teamster finally agreed to have me apologize. He came over and met with me, Paul Jennings, and the unit production manager. I said, "I'm sorry that I put my hand on you and said what I did," and he didn't accept my apology. By turning down my apology, his message was screw you, I beat you, you're going home. After the teamster left, I looked at Paul and said "What else do you want me to do here?"

The next day on the set, the unit production manager and Paul Jennings came over and sat down. I said, "Are we good? Is everything fine?"

The unit production manager said, "No. Warner Brothers is now involved. The teamsters called the studio, and if you're not fired, they're threatening to shut down the production."

I'd never been fired off a job from as far back as when I picked lemons for Sunkist when I was in high school. I said to the unit production manager, "I'll tell you what I'll do. I'll quit. Does that make it better for you?" My sons were coming to visit. Joni and I had already bought their plane tickets.

The unit production manager was very nice. She said, "My hands are tied, Rick. I see what's happening here. It's like the mafia."

I said, "Okay, I'll quit, but before I do, can I do the crash that I was going to do tonight?" The crash was Jim Wilkey in a semi-truck coming in and taking out a bunch of stuntmen in cars. Later, Jimmy

With Tom Struthers.

and the rest of us did the crash and everything was great. As I got out of my car, Tom Struthers came over and made sure everyone was okay, paying special attention to me. "You good, mate?"

"Yeah, I'm good." Because I love Tom, I gave him my radio and a big hug and told him with an endearing smile that I quit. I never felt so good. That evening I walked the city streets of Chicago back to the hotel. Joni was incensed with what had happened because, of course, she got sent home, as well.

I was distraught for a long time. Months passed, and then I heard that Chris Nolan was set to direct *Inception* (2010) that was being shot in Los Angeles. Tom Struthers was hired as the stunt coordinator, and when I didn't hear from him, I strongly suspected that I'd burned a major bridge.

A few years after *Inception* was completed, I ran into Tom Struthers. After our initial greetings, I said, "Tom, I'm sorry. Looking back on my leaving *The Dark Knight*, I know exactly what happened.

Joni and I were having serious marital problems. That doesn't excuse what happened, but as a friend, it's important that you know the whole story."

Tom looked surprised. "I'm sorry, Rick. I didn't know that. A lot of people were asking 'What's with Rick? He's not like he was on the last couple of movies.'"

"Well, that's what it was. My personal life was in the shitter." This was a true statement. I wasn't making this up.

"Oh, well, mate, I'm getting ready to do the next Batman—*The Dark Knight Rises.* Let me talk to Chris."

Tom talked with Chris Nolan, who said I could come back. I'd worked for Warner Brothers since quitting *The Dark Knight,* so I knew I wasn't outright blacklisted. What surprised me was that Chris was fine with hiring me onto another Warner Brothers Batman movie, given that he almost got shut down in Chicago because of me.

Reliving the first night I showed up on the set to do a car chase brings tears to my eyes. This shot involved a police car, the Bat motorcycle, and the villain's motorcycle. Throughout the first two Batman movies, scores of police cars were chasing the Bat Mobile, and on many of those chases I was the number one police car. If not number one, I was number two or number three.

When I saw Chris Nolan and Wally Pfister, who was the director of photography and an old friend, I hid behind the stunt guys. I didn't want Chris and Wally to see me because I didn't know what their reaction would be. I just wanted to be invisible so that I wouldn't ruin my first day back on Batman.

When they saw me, Wally came over and was just as sweet as he could be. And Cory, his key guy, came over and said, "Hey, Rick, it's great to see you back." And then Chris Nolan came over and said jokingly, "Hey, Rick, welcome back. Where'd you park?" So he remembered.

What was truly moving, however, was Tom Struthers said,

"Okay, Rick, get in that police car over there," which was the first police car. They put me back right where I left off. It was wonderful closure on that bad chapter. It was a nice reunion. My harsh quitting years earlier coupled with the unconditional warm welcome I received when I came back made me feel like the prodigal son of the stunt world.

I've rarely had any fear of performing on a movie set and have never been intimidated by movie stars. Except for the early stages of my career, I've felt much at home working on a film and being around film people. Moreover, I've never minded being the beneficiary of a good laugh, like the time I worked with Mel Gibson on the mystery drama *Edge of Darkness* (2010).

Besides doing stunts, on the first day, 007 director Martin Campbell gave me a small part playing Mr. Robinson Jr. that resulted in me and Mel fighting. This wasn't Woody Allen I'd be fighting. This was multitalented, action superstar Mel Gibson, who often played angry or deranged characters.

The morning Mel arrived on the set, I was sitting at a table where, in the scene, he was going to come over and we were to exchange a line of dialogue. As he got closer to the table, I could hear him talking with people in that rich, gravelly voice that seemed more menacing than I recalled in his movies.

When he finally arrived in front of me, I thought I'd offer a friendly, and perhaps clever, introduction. "Hi, Mel, I'm Rick Avery," I said, shaking his hand with a smile. "I worked with you years ago on *The River* when we were both young and handsome." Without hesitation, Mel replied, "Well, what the fuck happened to you?" The roar of laughter was deafening, and I was one of those laughing the hardest.

Mel and I spent the rest of the day trading banter and having a great time pounding on each other. Unlike his character roles, he was one of the most relaxed actors I've ever worked with, and that day was

Acting Mr. Robinson, Jr.

one of the most fantastic days I've spent in the movie business. Perhaps the greatest surprise was when he mentioned that he was born in Peekskill, New York and that in all likelihood as children we swam in the same lake!

If any actor tops Mel Gibson's cold, lethal stare, it would arguably be Robert De Niro, who is revered as one of the greatest actors in the history of Hollywood filmmaking. I first worked with Bob on the action crime drama *Heat* (1995) that costarred Al Pacino. I had a part in the beginning of the movie as an armored car guard where an armored truck I'm riding in is crashes into by a second semi-tow truck driven by Gary "The Wiz" McClarty. Two thugs drag me from my vehicle after it rolled over, and, in what became a famous scene, I'm subsequently shot in the forehead by a man in a hockey mask.

The second time I worked with Bob was on *Casino* where Joe

19 INT. ARMORED VAN - DRIVER'S POV: THE STREET + DISTANT 19
   AMBULANCE

Its FLASHERS light up. It signals. Slowly, safely, it pulls
across the street as if trying a three point turn because it
received a call. It appears normal. (Chris and Neil now wear   *
webbing vests.) Driver of the armored van brakes. Meanwhile:

20 INT. 14-WHEELER - CERRITO 20

winding through the gears.

CERRITO POV: ARMORED VAN IN PROFILE

We're driving right at it.

CERRITO'S FOOT

punches the accelerator.

FRONTAL: 14-WHEELER

dwarfing passenger cars, its double steel bumpers - a huge,
charging, metal beast.

CERRITO'S POV: JAMMING *85062*

at the Armored Van.

20A INT. ARMORED VAN - DRIVER 20A *

frantically trying to downshift, shouting, when...   *

20B INT. ARMORED VAN - MOMENT OF COLLISION 20B *

We SLAM into it.   *

WIDE: ARMORED VAN   *

shoved sideways across #1 lane to the curb. The curb trips it   *
onto its side.   *

21 INT. ARMORED VAN - DRIVER'S - DAY 21

world is knocked sideways. It rains paper. Guards thrown
against the ceiling.

21A EXT. T-JUNCTION - ARMORED VAN 21A

on its side plowing through parking meters, ripping up pavement.

22 OMITTED 22 *

Acting in *Heat*.

Pesci beat me up in an alley. Pesci is a method actor, so when he wailed on me with a huge trash can lid, I moved my elbow around and took the punishment on my pads. Moments later, when he was kicking me on the ground, I rolled on my side to again absorb his hard kicks on my pads.

After each take, Joe asked me if I was all right. I don't think he knew that I was wearing pads. When I kept telling him I was fine, I think he took this as a chal-

With Joe Pesci.

lenge and began hitting and kicking me harder.

The third time I worked with De Niro was when I was hired to double Dustin Hoffman on *Meet the Fockers* (2004). I had a tackle scene to do with Bob's stuntman, as well as some minor driving and a kicking scene. The kick the director wanted me to do was a martial arts kick that misses Bob's face and ends up kicking Ben Stiller's face. We were standing in sand, and after I'd rehearsed it, Bob came over, and when I threw the kick, I inadvertently kicked sand in Bob's face. I could have died right there on the spot.

"Oh my, Mr. De Niro, I'm so sorry."

For what seemed an eternity, he gave me that infamous silent stare with all the impending rage of Jake La Motta in *Raging Bull* and Max Cody in *Cape Fear*. Finally, he said, "No, that's fine. That's very impressive."

Whew!

No stuntman's story would be complete without at least one memorable encounter with the incomparable Judo Gene LeBell. I was working the comedy-drama *Article 99* (1992) with John McGin-

LeBell vs. Liotta.

ley, Forest Whittaker, Keifer Sutherland, and Ray Liotta.

The director, Howie Deutch, needed a character-faced stuntman to deal with some Dobermans on the show, and in my view no one fit that bill better than Gene LeBell, who is considered by many to be the toughest man alive.

Gene is a famous judo man, who did mixed martial arts (MMA)

before mixed martial arts existed. Universally respected by Muhammad Ali, world champion kickboxer Benny Urquidez, and kung-fu action movie star Bruce Lee, Gene has never been beaten. When his name is mentioned in conversation, the stories go on for hours. Everyone has a Gene story.

I was on the set of *Men in Black 2* (2002 action, adventure, comedy) and saw stunt people were lining up to have Gene choke them out (he's famous for that), just so they could say it happened.

Today, Gene is in his 80s and has worked as one of "Rowdy" Rhonda Rousey's trainers and is always in her corner. Gene rarely dresses sharp, wears a pink gi when working out, and uses a lackluster suitcase to carry his stunt pads. He has the overall look of the Maytag repairman. I love him.

Two days later, Gene arrived to play the part. Ray Liotta was standing next to me when I casually pointed to Gene and asked, "Do you know who that is?" I had coordinated for previously for Ray on my first stunt coordinator job given to me by Alan Gibbs. The TV series, *Our Family Honor*, was filmed in New York City and starred Eli Wallach.

"No," Ray replied.

"That's Gene LeBell, the toughest man in the world."

Ray looked at Gene and laughed, "No way."

I called Gene over to meet Ray. After we chatted for a couple of minutes, I mentioned to Ray that Gene was so tough that no one could choke him out. When Ray said he didn't believe me, Gene challenged Ray to try to choke him. Ray didn't want to, but Gene egged him on.

Ray put both hands on Gene's neck and in a gentlemanly way tried choking Gene, who laughed and told Ray to try harder. The harder Ray tried, the louder Gene laughed. While being unsuccessfully choked, Gene told an onlooker to get an apple box, so Ray could stand on it and try putting all his weight into it. Ray isn't a small man. Despite the apple box and trying as hard as he could, Ray was chided by Gene, who said to him, red face and all, "Is that all you got, pussy?"

Ray gave up, impressed and now a believer. Then Gene, ever the showman, said to me, "Show him how, Rick." I reached up put one hand on Gene's neck to choke him, and he gasped in pain while throwing himself to the floor. Ray looked at me, not believing what he just saw. Gene, always the gentleman, made me look good.

One major aspect that has kept me working in the Hollywood film industry is the total unpredictability of the dynamic people I meet, as well as when, where, and how they may appear in world headlines. In 1994, I worked on a TV adventure drama series called *Frogmen* starring O.J. Simpson.

For years, I'd been a huge fan of O.J. Who wasn't? We had a scene to do off a boat at night in San Pedro. Before we did the shot, I came into the boat's pilothouse with a football and asked O.J. if he'd sign it for me, which he graciously did. The following morning, just as the sun came up, O.J. and I did a tussle on the deck of the boat that ended with him lifting me overhead and throwing me overboard into the San Pedro Harbor.

A few months later, I was in my hotel room in Tel Aviv, Israel, going over cast videos for a movie I was set to direct when the car chase with O.J.'s white Bronco came on TV—even in Israel! Because I was a huge admirer of O.J., I followed his unfolding trial. As the trial heated up, I wondered if I was going to be called as a prosecution witness to discredit the defense's claim that O.J. had a bad shoulder. I envisioned someone from the prosecutor's office getting wind of O.J. lifting me overhead and throwing me overboard, which surely would have been problematic for the defense's position that O.J. had a bad shoulder and couldn't lift his arms above his chest. For whatever reason, I was never contacted.

Unpredictability comes in many forms, including things that can dramatically go haywire while shooting an action scene. In the same year that O.J. threw me into the San Pedro Harbor, I worked as a stuntman on the biographical drama TV movie *Out of Darkness* starring Diana Ross. The film was about Paulie Cooper, a former med student who becomes ill with paranoid schizophrenia and loses 18 years of her life.

Because I was known in the business as an ex-cop, I got a lot of small parts playing a police officer and still do. Jeannie Epper was the stunt coordinator, and for a simple gag, she had me there for a reason.

Stunt people are often brought into a film to do only one scene and given no background as to what the movie is about. All Jeannie told me was that the scene was at night in the rain and that Diana Ross would be in an alley on her knees crying when I arrived in my police car to arrest her.

While Jeannie was explaining this to me on the set, Diana's bodyguard, a monster size African American man, was listening and glaring at me. I didn't understand why until Jeannie added that Diana would be naked holding her upper garments to her chest. My job, Jeannie said, was to use all of my police expertise to arrest her and bring her to my patrol car without exposing her breasts.

After a brief peaceful, low key rehearsal, the director yelled, "Action!" I left my patrol unit in the alley and walked to Diana who was on her knees, sobbing in the rain. When I reached down to stand her up, she started to fight with me, which included kicking. We didn't rehearse this full speed, and I wasn't prepared for how strong this small woman was.

I grabbed her from behind, trying to keep her under control, and held the top to her as best I could. It was an all-out struggle and her top was coming off. Suddenly, my hands were on her nipple and I spotted her bodyguard inching closer with a murderous glare. I got her to the hood of the police car, which she used to push off. My hands were now all over her breasts, trying to keep them covered. Finally, I was greatly relieved and grateful to hear the word "Cut!"

A half hour later, Diana and her Sasquatch bodyguard got in their awaiting limo and drove off. For all her trouble, Diana was nominated for a Golden Globe, and I was rewarded by her bodyguard not kicking my ass.

Diana Ross wasn't my only embarrassing scene. I had my entire head buried in Pamela Anderson's crotch while she sat in a car during a chase sequence that had my legs dangling furiously from one of the car's side windows. After a big stair fall on *V.I.P.*, Pamela ended up standing over me in a short skirt.

It all sounds good after the fact, but it was monumentally embarrassing at the time. I'm as healthy as the next guy when it comes to these types of scenes with female actors, especially stars, but I get embarrassed and feel bad for them.

My all-time worst embarrassing scene in all the TV shows and movies I've made over the past 36 years occurred on the hit TV series *Knight Rider*. The gag was I was doubling an actor who gets hit by a car that was backing up fast. Because I was heavier than the actor, I had a hard time fitting into his pants. As planned, the car driven by the stunt guy accelerated back into me, and I fell to the ground. David Hasselhoff was on the set, and after I got hit, the crew was applauding, as they often do after a good stunt.

I got up and looked at the crew, who wouldn't stop applauding. It went on and on until I finally looked down and saw why. Those tight pants had ripped when I was hit by the car and Mr. Winky was hanging out partially for all to see! Time to cross my legs and turn beet red. What was worse was the male wardrobe person came over and right on the set reached into my pants, which felt to me like he was double dipping, to tape them up for the second take. Hey, kid, can you sing, can you dance?

Chapter 13:

Tragedy Strikes

In 1993, my film career and my marriage were going fantastically. A few years earlier, when they came of age, Dianne and Brian came to live with me and Joni. In 1991, Dianne started work as a secretary at the Los Angeles Sheriff's Department and made me extremely proud that she was continuing in law enforcement where I left off. Brian lived with us and eventually graduated from College of the Canyons, studying graphic design. A year before he graduated, when he told me he wasn't going to continue with his education, I gave him a year's notice to find a place and plan his future.

Along with my son Mikey, our family did things together and were close. At that time, we were living in a new 2,500 square foot home in Newhall, my three children were blossoming and in excellent health, and for years I'd been consistently working or coordinating three shows at a time.

After all those years spent as a cop, coupled with my career of performing dangerous stunts for more than a decade, I felt there was

Top, me and Brian, a man now; middle, Dianne and Brian; bottom, Joni and I with the boys.

nothing life could throw at me that I couldn't handle. Then one day, Joni was driving our eight-year-old son Mikey home from school when he told her that he was having a hard time seeing.

"What do you mean, honey?" Joni asked.

Mikey rubbed his eyes, squinted several times, and then tilted his head at different angles.

"I don't know, Mom. It's like I'm looking through a tunnel or something."

Joni knew that Mikey wasn't playing games and could sense that he was scared. She drove to the nearest Doc in the Box (urgent care) and explained Mikey's symptoms to the attending physician. Suspecting what the problem was, the doctor ordered a blood test that confirmed his suspicions. In the blink of an eye, Mikey was diagnosed with Type 1 diabetes, which is a rare form of diabetes. Only five percent of people with diabetes have Type 1.

Later that day, a specialist, Dr. Smith, sat with Joni and me and explained that Mikey's condition was caused by his immune system having destroyed his body's ability to make insulin, which is needed to move glucose into his cells. Instead, the glucose builds up in our son's blood, causing his cells to starve. In turn, this causes high blood sugar, which can lead to many problems, some being life threatening.

There are few things in the life of a parent that are worse than not being able to help their child who is confused and physically suffering. I was devastated by this feeling of total helplessness. Over my many years of being a cop, I'd done my best to protect and serve, and in many cases saved lives. My young son looked up to me. I was his hero, his Superman. But now I couldn't fight this battle for him and make his suffering go away.

In some ways, Mikey handled his illness better than I was able to. Children have a remarkable way of recovering emotionally, perhaps because they're still at that age where they live a day at a time. Joni and I, however, were looking at the full picture that, barring a cure,

Joni and Mikey.

was of Mikey having to live with being a Type 1 diabetic for the rest of his life.

The doctor immediately admitted Mikey to the hospital. To see this little eight-year-old in his child-sized hospital smock getting probed and prodded and stuck with needles totally took me out of my realm. The first night Joni stayed with him at the hospital, I got in my truck in the parking lot and crawled up in a ball and broke down and sobbed.

A few days later, we brought Mikey home. Prior to leaving the hospital, the medical staff taught us how to give our son an insulin shot and how to check his blood sugar level. Because a diabetic is constantly at risk of crashing, we had to monitor Mikey's blood glucose/insulin levels a half dozen times a day.

The nights were far worse because unless Joni and I woke Mikey by sticking him with a needle, he would sleep for eight hours with only our visual monitoring. I soon became a victim of sleep deprivation because I'd go to sleep worrying that my son's insulin level could drop so low during the night that he'd fall into a coma and die. This was even harder on Joni.

Hours later, I'd awaken drenched in sweat and go to Mikey's room and study his color, listen to his breathing, and feel his skin temperature. For the first time in my life, I stopped looking forward to going to bed at night.

After six months, Joni and I became proficient at detecting the signs that our son's numbers were off. The reason physicians sometimes refer to diabetes as Well's Disease is because the diabetic becomes abnormally thirsty and can't drink enough fluids. This telltale sign was evident before we knew about Mikey's diabetes because we'd find empty cans of diet soda all over the house. If only we'd known, perhaps we could have addressed our son's illness earlier.

After a year of monitoring Mikey's blood sugar, we made a game out of it. When a diabetic is going low, one of the first signs is they can't process information. So we agreed on a key question, which was "What is Michael Jordan's number?" If Mikey didn't immediately respond with "twenty-three," then his mom and I knew his numbers were off, and that he could be crashing, which could lead to unconsciousness, coma, and death.

There were a number of times that Mikey crashed. By the grace of God, we were able to save him by placing sugar under his tongue because the only good thing about diabetes is the quick fix of sugar, which can be a candy bar, a glass of orange juice, or a soda. When this quick fix didn't work, we had an emergency kit in our refrigerator and would give him a glucagon shot. While this shot saved him, it would make him sick for 24 hours.

Mikey's diabetes defined a change in the upbringing of our son. If I would discipline him or ground him for misdeeds that kids do, after an hour or two his mom would say, "Okay, don't you think that's enough?"

I'd reply, "No. I realize he has a problem right now, but he needs to grow up as a man."

I have no doubt that this conflict added strain to our marriage. How severely this negatively impacted our relationship is difficult to guess. We put our child first and stepped up to the plate because that's how we have always been as parents.

Fourteen years later on Christmas morning of 2007, our living room was covered with presents awaiting my children Dianne, Brian, and Mikey (now 22 years of age). The phone can sometimes be a harbinger of bad news and this day was an example. Mikey's beautiful girlfriend Jelly called to tell us that she had brought Mikey to the emergency room. Earlier, when she came to his condo to pick him up for Christmas, she found him unconscious. My wife and I raced to the hospital.

When I arrived, I came to an immediate stop. I've seen this all before. Like a bad recurring dream. My young son Michael lying before me, his face pale and gaunt. His cheeks sallow. His breathing is rapid, his eyes staring far away. He gazes up toward me from his hospital bed in the E.R. with a lazy, wandering, unfocused eye, which lends an eeriness to his handsome face.

Many times over the years, he had passed out and gone into coma. I was always scared, and over the years, we'd always been able to revive him. This time, however, he wasn't only near comatose, but near death. The doctor said Mikey's body was actually feeding on itself, and he had gone into kidney failure.

Back at home, our son's gifts remained unopened under our tree. His year-old daughter, Bailey, waited there, wondering where Daddy was. Although he was mostly unaware of his surroundings, I know he recognized me because he managed a slight smile as I joined his mother, who has always been there for him. A total feeling of help-lessness brought tears to my eyes, as I leaned over and kissed her.

My son Michael has been a Type 1 diabetic since he was eight years old. Thirteen years of needles to date. His normal blood sugar should be between 70 and 130. It is now 1500. If he had not been found by his girlfriend, he would have died within two to three hours. As it stands now, the possibility looms darkly above us, as his body shuts down.

I glanced at a tattoo on his lower back. Seven years earlier while I was working in Mexico as a stunt coordinator on the movie *Blow*, Joni and Mikey (then age 15) decided to get matching tattoos. They both knew this was against my wishes, and when I found out what they had done, I was fuming mad. But now it was beyond insignificant.

His blood pressure is extremely high, and I can see the pulse throughout his lean muscular body as his body feeds on itself to stay alive.

Over the years, it was our small child Mikey who would be lying there. All we knew then was panic and tears. It was no easier now that he was an adult with a muscular body of a full grown man. I could

Mikey worked the sliding decks of *Titanic*.

hardly believe that only a few weeks earlier, he was working with me sliding down a deck on the set of the movie *Poseidon*. A young man who, when he was ten-years-old, was the only stunt child sliding down the decks on the movie *Titanic*, and at the age of three was the youngest person in the world to work on a stunt contract when he appeared in the Stan Winston movie *A Gnome Named Gnorm*.

This day in the hospital was one of the worst days of my life. Everything I'd worked for—my career, my home, my physical possessions, my bank account, and my pension—now all seemed totally worthless. I would have given it all back, as well as my own life, if somehow the powers that be would get Mikey through this. My prayers were heard and answered because within two days, Mikey had returned to normal.

We encountered another major tragedy when on January 17, 1994 at 4:30 in the morning, the Northridge earthquake struck. Although the earthquake was called the Northridge earthquake, its epicenter was in Reseda, which was 20 miles from our home in Santa Clarita.

This was no minor shaker. The 6.7 magnitude blind thrust earthquake had a ground acceleration that was the highest ever instrumentally recorded in an urban area in North America, with strong ground motion felt as far away as Las Vegas, Nevada. This was the first earthquake with a hypocenter directly beneath a U.S. city since the 1933 Long Beach earthquake.

I didn't know it at the time, but our house was built on fill, which is considerably less compacted than natural earth. Joni couldn't sleep that night, and at 4:30 in the morning was downstairs, having finally fallen asleep watching television. Upstairs, I was jarred from sleep by our house being shaken vertically. I thought World War III had started.

I ran from our bedroom and raced down the hall to the kids' bedrooms. While I was running to Mikey's bedroom and falling repeatedly to my knees, downstairs the whole TV console, which was a massive piece of furniture, crashed in front of Joni. She later told me that she'd heard screaming and didn't know where the screaming was coming from, and then realized it was her. In the adjacent garage, our truck was bouncing around so violently that it tried to come through the garage wall into our family room.

When I entered Mikey's bedroom, I went to lift him from his bed, and his furniture fell on my back. It was like a movie. When the initial 15-second quake struck, one minute after it ended, the first aftershock hit with a magnitude of 6.0. My older son, Brian, to escape from the house, kicked out his window on the second floor and climbed out. Ten minutes later, which felt like an eternity, all of us had managed to escape from the house.

Our home had a view of the Santa Clarita Valley, and the first thing I noticed when I got outside was how beautiful the sky looked. I stood in awe, wondering why I was seeing all the stars. The reason was that all the lights were out—everywhere. Meanwhile, loud explosions were going off, the biggest ones coming from electrical transformers situated high up on telephone poles. On our street, a huge river flowed down both lanes like a tsunami. This river was caused by the splitting of a giant reservoir tank that was situated atop an adjacent mountain.

Everyone lost electricity for quite a while before it was restored. Initially, we had no idea how far the quake went. Were we on the outside perimeter of a much greater earthquake like the 1906 San Francisco earthquake that had an estimated "moment magnitude" of 7.8? Had our Northridge earthquake completely leveled downtown Los Angeles? Were all our friends and relatives living within a hundred miles of us safe?

Eleven hours later, the second massive 6.0 aftershock hit, and would be followed by thousands more over the next week. It got to the point where our family could estimate the size of these aftershocks. Threes were ignored. Fours got honorable mention. Oh, that's just a five. At times, they arrived in waves, and then there would be hours without a single tremor. This never-knowing if another major earthquake was about to hit resulted in our living with the proverbial "waiting for the other shoe to drop" mindset. If there was any good news, we felt that the worst had passed. We had to.

The Army reserve brought large water trucks to the neighborhood. This was a time of bonding. When all the major cleanup was finished and life returned to normal, 57 people had lost their lives, with more than 8,700 injured. Additionally, earthquake-caused property damage was estimated to be between $13 and $40 billion, making it one of the costliest natural disasters in U.S. history.

We moved out of our house for a year because a construction crew had to literally rebuild our home from the ground up because the foundation was broken in three places. Professionals lifted the house with powerful hydraulics and reinforced the foundation with a hundred cubic yards of cement. The workers fixed that house so nicely, there was only one scratch on one wall, and the best news was our insurance company, State Farm, took care of everything.

A short while after life returned to normal, I began to notice the downside of film work. With all its excitement and allure, when I was on the road, I was spending a life away from my life. My existence became simplistic. I didn't own anything when on the road—no car, no motorcycle, not a lot of clothes except for what I could pack into two suitcases, no easy chair, and no family. I could add appreciably to this list. To make matters worse, sometimes location shoots would go on for months.

Secondly, as I became a seasoned stuntman, I didn't want to be hitting the ground as much or yanked into a wall by two guys pulling on a wire, which they might do a half-dozen times on any particular day. Across the boards, stunt work was becoming a hard way to make a living.

I'd go back to my hotel room and have to show up the next day to do something just as hard on my body, or worse. A stuntman does that for 10, 15, 20 years and they're battered like an NFL linesman. Doing stunts was no longer joyful like the first time I did it when I worked with John Travolta on *Blow Out*.

Another problem with working as a stuntman and becoming successful is one of moderation. The job of a stuntman or stunt coordinator isn't a typical nine-to-five. Crew hours on a standard feature film are a minimum of 12 hours, and I've worked as many as 18 hours on countless productions.

When I began working in the movie and television business, I grabbed at anything and everything that came my way. I didn't turn down any job. This was because for the first several years as my career grew, there were long droughts without work. I never got over this thirst. Even when I became successful, I didn't want to turn down work for fear that another slow period could be lingering on the horizon—or I could get injured and be laid up for months.

The problem comes when that slow period doesn't arrive, because the longer I went with no slow period in sight, the more convinced I became that I'd be out of work tomorrow. I've worked 24 hours a day for three consecutive days on three different shows for this reason. In my early days, I catnapped in the honey wagon or my car just to build my resume, reputation, and bank account.

If there is any truth to the old adage that bad things come in threes, I'm a testament to that.

One day, I'd been working hard for 13 hours flying a news helicopter over the Sylmar fire, and when I walked into the 4,400 square foot house that I considered my castle for 12 years, I instantly sensed that something was different. Within a matter of ten minutes, I discovered that all of Joni's personal things were gone. Without warning, she had abruptly ended our 33-year relationship.

I was utterly devastated and immediately fell into a deep depression that progressively seemed to get worse. I felt like the Bible's Job, who had always felt the uncertainly and instability of earthly things, and now cried out, "What I feared the most is upon me." All that I had worked so hard for—Joni and our children, our families, our personal possessions—everything that was once "ours" was no more.

Night after night, I cried myself to sleep, and would even get caught up in a fit of intense sobbing during the day. In an attempt to make sense of what had happened, I scoured the Internet and talked with a half dozen relationship experts, friends, family, and even near-complete strangers—anyone who would listen and might have an answer, and even better, a solution.

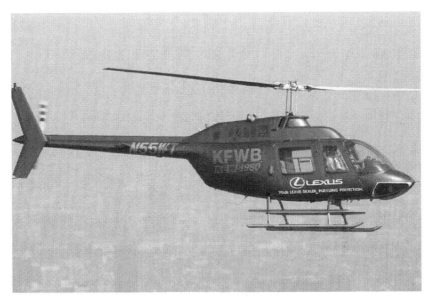

Sylmar fire.

For years, people told Joni and me how beautiful a couple we were and how they looked up to us as the model stunt couple of our industry. As hard as I tried, I found no answers. As much as I desperately wanted to fix our marriage, we were finished.

Had my childhood feelings of inadequacy been real all the time? Had I managed only to hide this inadequacy from her for years, and now she'd come to believe that I really wasn't the person she thought I was and left?

For the longest time, I thought I'd never get over my deep depression and sorrow. And then total relief came in the form of a miracle. I'd been involved in music since high school and have always felt that music is the closest connection between the universe and my soul. Then one afternoon, I was lying on the floor of my home, sobbing, when I overheard music playing from another room. The words, seemingly directed to me, were from this song by John Mayer.

"The Heart of Life"

I hate to see you cry
Laying there in that position
There's things you need to hear
So turn off your tears
And listen

Pain throws your heart to the ground
Love turns the whole thing around
No, it won't all go the way it should
But I know the heart of life is good

You know it's nothing new
Bad news never had good timing
But then the circle of your friends
Will defend the silver lining

Pain throws your heart to the ground
Love turns the whole thing around
No, it won't all go the way it should
But I know the heart of life is good

Pain throws your heart to the ground
Love turns the whole thing around
Fear is a friend who's misunderstood
But I know the heart of life is good
I know it's good.

From the moment I heard those words, a peace came over me that put me on the road to recovery. My getting over Joni was like a slow-melting iceberg that melts unnoticed a little each day. Weeks, even months pass, and one doesn't notice any change in the iceberg. And then one day, they suddenly notice that the iceberg doesn't carry the weight it did before.

Similarly, one morning I awoke and said, "My, I don't feel depressed today. In fact, I feel pretty good!"

Behind my house is a 3,700-foot mountain that one summer was burned to ash by the Sylmar fire, with not a single blade of grass surviving. In the hope of healing my soul, I decided I would try to climb the steepest part every day. . .

As the weeks passed, one day I spotted a tiny blade of grass and poured some of my drinking water on it to help it grow—just as I needed to do. During the Sylmar fire, aircraft dropped Foschek fire

I found these shovels on my first hike up the mountain . . . abandoned.

retardant on the mountain. Afterwards, the mountain was seeded by aircraft. Because of this process, eventually, my hikes were through six to eight feet of spring flowers above my head—evidence that the mountain was healed—and so was I.

In the end, I discovered that Joni' leaving had little to do with my being adequate or inadequate. My mistake was that I had placed far too much importance on myself.

Flowers above my head.

Thank you John Mayer for seeing me through. My heartfelt gratitude is owed to another person, but I'm getting ahead of myself. I'm living proof to the age-old wisdom of "When God closes one door, He opens another." In my case, the door that God opened led me on a path to a wonderful woman. When she enters the room, all eyes go to her, as she moves her body with a casual air of confidence. She is worldly and wise. Because she comes from New Jersey Irish stock, there is a toughness behind the beauty that lends itself to the talent and courage that won her Junior Olympic Gold and international championships in competitive springboard and tower diving.

Moviegoers know her as the iconic stuntwoman who hung from the helicopter in *True Lies* or the unforgettable scene in *Indiana Jones and the Temple of Doom* blasting off a cliff on a raft and landing in class 5 rapids. Her name is Donna Keegan who, along with John Mayer, helped get me through this difficult period.

I'd been in a blue funk for six months when one night I was on Facebook and saw the name Donna Keegan, a fellow stunt person. Over the years, we'd worked together, although most recently, five years earlier on the John Cusack, Ray Liotta movie *Identity*. Because Donna was married and been living in Tucson for several years, we'd lost touch.

After messaging back and forth for a week, we talked on the phone and eventually met for dinner at a Japanese sushi restaurant. I shared with her what had happened in my life and where I was.

Smiling again.

At the time, I had no idea that she'd been going through a similarly painful divorce and was presently living in a penthouse apartment with all her personal belongings, her son, and her two dogs. This is how she is, to a fault—she puts others first. We became close that night, and over the next six months, we gradually became romantically involved.

Although Donna is an exceptionally beautiful woman, I've learned that what is most important is a person's heart, and Donna has the biggest heart in the world. Because of her compassion, unique wisdom, life experience, and keen perception, she helped me get through my depression. In all my years, I've never met anyone like her. She is truly a treasure to behold.

She is also the most giving person I've ever known. She'll learn about something that someone she cares for likes, and then she'll make sure they get it. She'll go out of her way to help people to the point of hurting herself or inadvertently allowing them to hurt her. She abhors injustice and gets upset when she sees anyone in pain, and especially those who are the victim of someone else's wrongdoing.

Part of my healing process of getting through the end of my marriage was Donna took me to a place in Hollywood called The Magic Castle, which is a nightclub for magicians and magic enthusiasts, as well as the clubhouse for the Academy of Magical Arts. It was here that I made good use of a group of lessons that Donna had gifted to me that eventually resulted in my becoming a full-fledged magician member of The Magic Castle.

Donna is an extraordinarily driven woman in everything she does. Besides being a legend and icon as a stunt woman, she was respected

Donna and I at The Magic Castle with Mark Wilson.

in the Screen Actors Guild when she was the National Chairperson of Stunt and Safety; and when she decided to produce her documentary *Santa Monica: A Community of Caring*, which is a public service video for the American Heart Association, she won the highly-coveted Emmy Award for directing.

Since we began dating, Donna and I have become an inseparable team. She came on to help me produce Hardknocks.tv, and our days are filled with being creative. When I got the call to do *Hands of Stone*, Donna, of course, came with me.

A couple of years ago when we were dating, we were on the same shoot in Panama, and one night she said, "What are you going to do about me?"

Realizing she was broaching the subject of marriage, I replied, "I love you. Why can't we just continue the way we are? We'll live together and we'll be happy. We've both been married before, and more than once, and we failed at it. Why would we do it again? Let's just be happy."

But I knew she was right. Settling on living together is settling on a half-baked relationship. If we truly wanted to enjoy our relationship to its fullest potential, then we needed to make a lifelong commitment to each other. So after several years of dating and living together, upon our return from Panama, we drove to the Beverly Hills courthouse and exchanged our marriage vows.

Ours is a mature marriage that gets better with time. I don't relate to the words soulmate and helpmate to best describe our relationship. I see our relationship as rooted in a deep mutual respect.

Donna comes from working stock. Her father served during World War II and afterwards drove oil tankers for a living. She went from maid to New York City model and eventually to a brilliant stunt career, winning the Icon of the Year award presented by her peers.

Because she was also mentored by Alan Gibbs, she is compassionate about my feelings toward him. Today, she has a fantastic management company and is highly respected in the entertainment industry, as well as the professional boxing profession.

She also can predict the end of a story on TV or a movie ten minutes in. "Stop! Stop!" I will yell. She is always right and wide-eyed, and will look at me with a knowing smile to not spoil it.

Donna is an executive chef, having graduated from Le Cordon Bleu. What is uncanny is her talent to taste with her mind. She'll ask me, "Why don't you like that dish? Is it the texture, the spice, too gooey, how it looks?" Then she will totally customize for my taste. Awesome! My own personal chef, ooh la la!

Donna has been by my side and concerned about me for a long time. When I did the Ferrari roll over for Dr. Dre's video "I Need a Doctor," she came to watch with her son Gary, whom I've known since he was 14 years of age.

Gary strongly resembles Johnny Depp, but stands 6'2". We've watched Gary grow as a young writer, actor, and director. He studies acting at Stella Adler in Hollywood and is growing into a fine young man who will grow into the film world.

His natural ability amazes us. At the young age of 15, he played the part of Thenardier in *Les Miserables* at a playhouse in Hollywood. Wearing a skull cap with a comb over hair piece and a pot belly body suit, he stole the show. He has comedic timing and mannerisms we liken to that of Jim Carrey.

In August 2010, we took a fun filled 3-day adventure trip in our plane to San Francisco. Donna and Gary love to fly. I'm happy to say we saw all the sights, including Alcatraz.

I have an enormous amount of admiration for my wife and the fact that she's a great visionary and hard worker who gets things done. We've grown closer together over the years, and I see a wonderful future for the two of us.

Chapter 14:

To Touch
the Face of God

John Gillespie Magee, Jr. was an aviator who served in the Royal Canadian Air Force. He died at the age of 19 in a mid-air collision over Lincolnshire in 1941. Magee's posthumous fame rests mainly on his sonnet *High Flight*, which he started just a few months before his death. In his seventh flight in a Spitfire Mk I, he had flown up to 33,000 feet. As he orbited and climbed upward, he was struck by words he'd read in another poem — "To touch the face of God." He completed his verse soon after landing.

Portions of the poem appear on many of the headstones in the Arlington National Cemetery. Astronaut Michael Collins brought an index card with the poem typed on it on his Gemini 10 flight. Over the years, I've often reflected on these words that resonate with me and define a substantial part of my life:

High Flight

Oh, I have slipped the surly bonds of earth
And danced the skies on laughter-silvered wings;
Sunward I've climbed, and joined the tumbling mirth
Of sun-split clouds . . . and done a hundred things
You have not dreamed of . . . wheeled and soared and swung
High in the sunlit silence. Hov'ring there,
I've chased the shouting wind along, and flung
My eager craft through footless halls of air.
Up, up the long, delirious, burning blue
I've topped the windswept heights with easy grace
Where never lark, or even eagle flew.
And, while with silent, lifting mind I've trod
The high untrespassed sanctity of space
Put out my hand, and touched the face of God.

During my childhood, one of my favorite TV shows was *Sky King*. To this day, I can recall the opening to television's premier aviation program, "From out of the clear blue of the western sky comes Sky King." Operating from his Flying Crown Ranch in Arizona, Sky King, his niece Penny, and their Cessna 310 airplane "Songbird" were involved in one adventure after another. Viewed by many children in the 1950s, this TV show inspired my love for aviation.

When my family went to Peekskill in the summer, I often played Army/Navy with my cousin Frankie. Years later, he became a Navy aviator and one weekend came to Santa Barbara when I was a young teenager and took me on a flight in a Cessna.

I immediately fell in love with flying, but at the time couldn't afford the expensive flying lessons. Then in the early-80s when my film career took off, I was able to pay for flying lessons that eventually led to my obtaining my private pilot's license. The first aircraft that I flew solo was a single engine Piper Tomahawk.

A friend, stuntman Mike DeLuna, called and said, "Hey, you've got a license to fly, don't you?" Mike was an ex-Golden Knight, which is a demonstration and competition parachute team of the United States Army.

"I'd fly without one, but yes," I replied jokingly.

My Cessna 182.

"We're doing a movie called *The Adventures of Buckaroo Banzai Across the 8th Dimension* and I have to jump out of a plane. Can you fly to LA and I'll jump out of your plane?"

"Sure, no problem."

I flew to Torrance Airport and Mike jumped out of my plane. Later that afternoon on my flight back to Santa Barbara, it occurred to me that maybe I could make a career flying for the movies. Over the next couple of years, I got my commercial license, my multi-engine license, and then my instrument multi-engine license.

Rick, Mikey, and Brian hanging; Craig Hosking pilot.

I was spending a lot of money renting airplanes and finally decided to purchase a Cessna Skylane 182. During this time, although I didn't receive any jobs flying for a production company, I got my friends to go places with me—usually fun stuff like flying 200 miles to have a hamburger at a famous burger joint.

When I ran out of fun things, I volunteered to fly for Air Lifeline and Angel Flight. I'd donate the gas and my time to fly low income people, who couldn't afford transportation, to medical facilities throughout the United States. I flew around 25 missions.

As far back as I can remember, the stuntmen have been the rock stars on the set. When a veteran cowboy gallops a horse hell-bent for leather and rides off a cliff and splashes down into a river, that's impressive. So are high speed car chases with their screeching tires and the cacophony of twisting metal when the cars collide.

These things, however, pale by comparison to when a helicopter arrives on the set with its mighty engine and its blades kicking up a powerful downdraft along with the familiar thump, thump, thump that literally shakes the ground. It's a similar feeling one gets when the Blue Angels make a low pass over the Super Bowl or a patriotic parade.

The first time I saw a helicopter set down at a film location, I wanted to be the guy flying that aircraft. In the early 1990s, there was only a small, select group of movie pilots working in the film and television industry—and I became determined to become one of them.

Almost immediately, I began attending classes and took hands-on flying instruction at a company called Group 3 Aviation. Within a year and a half, I obtained my private helicopter license, my commercial license, my instrument license, my CFI, and CFII. In a short period of time, I was asked to instruct. Accepting their offer, I taught for ten years and graduated 35 students up to instructional ratings.

Helicopters have two major advantages over airplanes. One, they can suddenly come to a complete stop in midair; and two, they can land practically anywhere on a moment's notice.

After I was teaching for a while, I was offered the opportunity to fly for the news, which allowed me to log a good deal of turbine time. I flew for KFWB News for two years, and then Dick Hart and Helen Kosmala gave me a job at National Helicopters. Eventually, I became the company's chief pilot and flew its A-Stars, which is a European turbine helicopter, and Jet Rangers. This was a gamble because word started getting around the film industry that Rick wasn't doing stunts anymore, but was flying helicopters for the news. This became problematic.

Eventually, I obtained work on movie productions flying camera ships, which was my dream from the beginning. Many movie shots that call for a helicopter involve stunt people. Because I'm both a helicopter pilot and a stuntman, this gave me a leg up. If an action shot required a stunt person to hang off a helicopter, the best case scenario would be to have a fellow stuntman flying the helicopter. For that reason, over the years many stunt coordinators have specifically requested that I fly the helicopter used in their aerial shots.

Rick flying Cineflex.

There are many forms of stunt helicopter work. One day, I might fly in a commercial with a PictorVision ball with a camera system mounted on the nose of the helicopter. A typical shot might be for me to fly radically high above a half-dozen cars, and then dive down and move among them like an Indy driver. Later in the week, I might work on a movie transporting its stars from point A to point B, which amounts to routine takeoffs and landings.

For many helicopter pilots who are new to flying for the movie business, the work can be dangerous, which is why there are movie pilots and regular pilots. Movie pilots are a rare cat. There are about ten of them who make their living doing nothing but flying helicopters for film and television companies. They've seen it all and done it all.

Stunt movie pilots are the best pilots in the world because everything they do is extreme. They constantly push their aircraft to its limits, flying at high altitudes, diving at insane speeds and angles, flying at night between high-rise buildings, having people hang and rappel from the chopper's skids. In many ways, movie pilots are much like combat pilots. They're both extraordinarily fearless and skillful.

One year I was flown to Hawaii to work on the production *Journey to the Center of the Earth 2*. The director wanted me to take off from a pier in a Jet Ranger. Because the helicopter was supposed to be old, the director wanted me to get the engine to backfire, and then fly the helicopter erratically. Any good pilot can make a helicopter look like it's out of control. But what I did was considered a stunt because the helicopter, and especially its tail rotor, was close to the crew.

Other times, I've been asked to fly head-ons just feet above on-coming cars. After a while, these sort of stunts become routine and are all in a day's work.

Guardian Helicopters was located at the same airport as National Helicopters and was known for its firefighting and lift work. In heli-copter lingo, lift work refers to a helicopter lifting a wide variety of loads that include massive buckets of water, boulders, people, and

Standing on a roof in downtown LA.

heavy machinery such as placing a commercial air conditioning on the roof a high-rise building. We've all seen the commercial that show a full-sized car sitting on the top of a mountain. It was put there by a helicopter.

I rarely had anything dangerous happen with a helicopter. Late one afternoon, however, I was training a commercial pilot to be an instructor. We were returning from the Fillmore area and were climbing over a mountain when he said, "Rick, I can't control the RPMs." This usually is the result of a mechanical error and is technically called an "over speed." The engine was out of control and sounded like a formula one race car. If it redlined for a long period, it could burn up and we could lose power and have to auto rotate to the ground.

I took the controls and said "Wow, I can't either. Stay calm." We were near the top of a mountain. There was no place to land, but we could gradually descend. I had the option of shutting the engine down, which I chose not to do. I wasn't going to shut down a perfectly running helicopter while its blades were turning. Besides that, there was a maze of wires below us. With the chopper's thunderous engine sounding like an F5 tornado, I kept flying until I found a spot to make an uneventful landing.

In the spring of 2013, the owner, Phil DiFiore, of Guardian Helicopters asked me if I'd be interested in flying during the upcoming fire season. I'd been watching these guys for years. Professional yet fun, they reminded me of stunt guys. I respected them and felt honored to have been asked. All else aside, this was right up my alley—fire, danger, and saving lives—and so I was unhesitatingly all in.

I committed to the entire fire season because the owners of Guardian invested considerable money training me to fight fires. Besides learning how to drop buckets of water onto forest fires, I needed additional certification.

I fought eight fires while I was with that company, including the notorious Rim Fire that was started on August 17, 2013 by a hunter's illegal campfire that got out of control. It was the third largest wildfire in California's history, having burned 257,314 acres.

The Rim Fire was an Armageddon fire. Everywhere I looked everything was ablaze. Firefighters battled that fire for nine weeks before it was fully contained, and more than a year passed before it was officially declared out. Thankfully, there were no fatalities, although ten firemen were injured. Putting out that fire cost more than $127-million.

Helicopter pilots who fight fires have two great fears. Because helicopters often fly at low altitudes, there's an increased danger when flying because unseen obstructions and wires can bring down the aircraft. The second is the fear of sudden engine failure (coupled with no safe place to make an immediate landing) because these pilots are pushing the helicopter to its limits.

The four variables that spell danger for a helicopter are known among aviators as "The Four H's"—High (as in altitude), Humid, Heavy, and Hot. I would also add to this list sudden, strong turbulence. When flying a helicopter to fight a forest fire, all five of these variables can come into play, and sometimes all at once.

Fighting a fire from the air over many hours is hot, arduous work. By the time I put my helicopter to bed and drove to my motel room and showered, I might get four hours of sleep before I'm heading back to resume the fight.

Helicopter pilots who battle forest fires have several different missions. The majority of the missions I flew were HELCO, IR, and RECON. When I was on a Helco mission, I flew with a fireman whose job it was to follow instructions from the air boss, who was in charge of the overall air attack.

The air boss flies an airplane at a high altitude and, based on what he sees, instructs the big tanker aircraft and helicopters below. The Helco fireman is in charge of all the helicopters that are on the fire. Together with this fireman, my job was to find hot spots and

Rim fire.

mark these on a map, and then bring in the helicopters and other aircraft—either by talking or guiding them in—and generally supervise
the water drops and/or offloading firemen.

RECON missions mainly involved checking out reported lightning strikes and making sure that previous hot spots were fully out.
This was necessary because often although from the air a fire looks
like it's out, it can still be burning. I'd fly in low and use infrared (IR)
technology to confirm the fire was completely extinguished.

I flew until what is called pumpkin time, which is sunset. I had to
return to the command base because the fire boss didn't want anyone
flying at night.

In a sense, these guys were putting their lives on the line and
fighting in combat. While true they weren't fighting enemy soldiers,
the fire they were up against could kill in a matter of minutes. By
my leaving at sunset, I was cutting off their water drops and Helco

connection. I felt terrible when ordered to return to base but, as was the case when I served in the Army, I followed orders.

Sandy Willett, who was my partner when I was a motorcycle cop for the Santa Barbara Police Department grew up as a pilot. He was from the small farm community of Willits in Northern California where his family were crop dusters. Sandy was such a good pilot, he would fly his crop duster to the aqueducts and stick the plane's tires into the water and wash the undercarriage of the aircraft as he flew back to the airport.

One day when I was a relatively new pilot, he took me flying in a T-6, which was a WWII trainer. He told me to take the stick and fly the aircraft for a while. After I flew for a few minutes like the pilot version of the "little old lady from Pasadena," Sandy took the controls and over the next five minutes scared the living daylights out of me — and I don't scare easily. Man, could he fly!

In later years, Sandy flew airplanes for the California Forestry

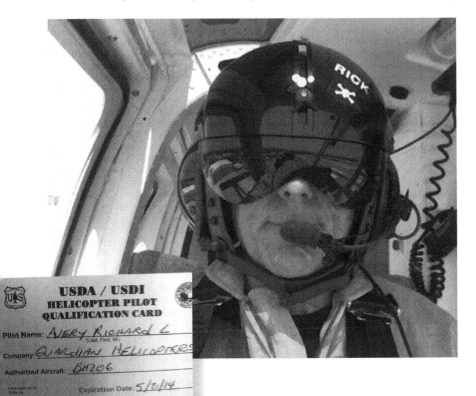

Service in much the same capacity that I did. He was killed while flying a reconnaissance flight over a dangerous area where three fires had been started by an arsonist. Because of this, whenever I flew over a raging forest fire, the memory of Sandy often resulted in tears welling up in my eyes.

Fighting fires is an extremely rewarding job because everybody—men, women, and children of all ages—loves a fireman. Those who fight fires charge into the face of danger while everyone else is running away. In sharp contrast, police often anger people, but not firemen. I'd walk into a restaurant, and when the patrons learned that I was flying on a fire, they'd validate me and pat me on the back like people did in my stunt work.

The following season I again helped fight California's wildfires. The third season I was asked to sign a three-month contract to fight forest fires in Wenatchee in north-central Washington, which my wife Donna convinced me to turn down because it would put on hold my other endeavors for too long. Thus ended my firefighting career, as much as I loved it.

Since being hired by John Travolta in 1978 to handle the security at his ranch, as well as his personal security, I've consistently sought out jobs that tend to change from day to day. Such was the case when I was working as a cop, as well as doing stunt work. This has also held true for my working as a pilot for National Helicopters.

When I'm flying helicopters, the job can change every week. I could get an assignment to do a survey of cell phone towers, which requires landing in highly remote places, which is challenging. The following week, I might get a call from the unit production manager of *The Bachelor*, asking that I land in the driveway of the Bachelor house and transport that season's bachelor and his date (or a group

Passengers Josh Hutcherson and Vanessa Hudgen.

With Gordon Ramsay.

date) to downtown Los Angeles and land on a high-rise rooftop. Then the next day, I could be doing a powerline survey or instructing a student pilot on how to do full power auto rotation landings.

By far, the most relaxing and fun part of flying helicopters is doing charter work. One day, I could be flying a group of wealthy people to the Coachella Valley for a music festival, which could cost them thousands (helicopter meters are far more severe than taxi cab meters

Bikini run.

or Uber drivers). And then the following day, I could be flying movie and sports celebrities.

One of my most memorable times was when I picked up L.A. Laker Julius Randall at LAX and flew him to Staples Center where he was playing in a game that evening. Because he was new to L.A., I took him on a tour of the beach communities and LA's suburban communities before dropping him off at Staples.

As I mentioned at the outset of this chapter, as far back as my childhood, I've been infatuated with aviation and have had an exhilarating love affair with flying. I'm not a believer in past lives, although I believe in the passing of DNA from generation to generation. As such, I'm convinced that someone in my DNA line was a pilot. I feel this way because the wonderment of flying resonates in my soul. I can sit at an airport beneath the wing of a plane and be totally content just sitting there.

Whenever I fly someone to LAX, my chosen return route is to fly to the beach and then fly 150 feet above the water. Pilots call this the "bikini run." I'm by myself doing the *Magnum PI* banking run over the ocean. I'm alone and feeling completely relaxed—and untouchable by the rest of the world—at least for a while. This feeling is beyond calming. It's almost like a rebirth. I am a pilot and blessed to live in the clouds every day I fly.

Chapter 15:

Directing

For many years, I aspired to work as a movie director. I carefully studied how directors set up a master shot and coverage shots. When given the opportunity, I looked through the various camera lenses to see composition and which size lenses did the best job for any particular scene. Over time, I learned about the different camera speeds, paying particular attention to slow motion and high speed for action sequences.

Movies should move. Even when the actors aren't moving, the viewer's point of view should keep changing to keep the audience interested. The easiest way to accomplish this is by cutting back and forth between the various coverage angles. With time, I learned the stock shots and angles, such as a pan, tilt, dolly shot, tracking shot, crane shot, zoom, low angle, high angle, Dutch angle, and also how to make the best use of a hand-held camera and Steadicam.

As a martial artist who spent countless hours watching the great action heroes, I was surprised when I first learned that action fight scenes are often shot at 22 frames per second instead of the normal 24 frames per second in order to make the actor appear faster and tighten up the scene. Sometimes even 20 frames per second is used. Car chases are usually shot at 20 frames per second in order to make the cars appear to be going faster, except if the cars are already moving at 100 mph as they were in *Batman Begins*. I educated myself for the day I got the opportunity. I'm a believer in the Oprah Winfrey wisdom of "You gotta be so good that when you get lucky, you're ready."

Movie production often requires the services of a second director. This additional director is called a second unit director, and the unit they oversee can be a small camera crew that shoots establishing shots and inserts—or it can be the same size as the as the first unit and shoot elaborate action sequences. As a general rule, second unit directors don't shoot scenes that include actors speaking dialogue.

Basically, the job of the second unit is to capture the scenes that the first unit doesn't have the time to shoot. Stuntmen and stunt coordinators are often asked to direct second units for movies and television.

My golden opportunity came in 1990 on the movie *DMZ*, which was a film about the demilitarized zone in the Korean War. The producer, Garret Vandermer, needed me to shoot an action sequence, and I was well prepared for the opportunity.

Actor Paul Sorvino asked me to direct him in a scene because he had a falling out with the director over creative differences. Although the movie was never released, my contract as a second unit director was honored by the Directors Guild of America (DGA) and my directing career was officially launched.

After *DMZ*, I was hired as a second unit director on 15 feature films. In 1995, I was working on an action film called *The Expert* starring Jeff Speakman and James Brolin. Bill Lustig was the director, and I was hired as the stunt coordinator, fight choreographer, and second unit director.

Bill Lustig (interestingly born and raised in the Bronx) had an out

First directing job wearing letterman's jacket.

of the ordinary early career, having directed a series of X-rated porn and gruesome slasher movies before teaming with fellow maverick independent filmmaker Larry Cohen. Together, they made a string of *Maniac Cop* hit movies that to this day have a substantial cult following.

One night, I was off the set while Bill was shooting when a production assistant called me over the radio and requested that I come to the set. When I arrived, the first assistant director asked me to take over a shot that was clearly Bill Lustig's.

It has always been sacrilege for a second unit director to do this. Essentially, it crosses an imaginary line. Bill was sitting ten feet from me, reading. When I asked why Bill wasn't directing the shot, the first assistant said, "Bill is having some kind of problem and we can't get him to say action."

I didn't know what to say and just stared into space, wishing I were elsewhere. "Rick, just say action so we can get this scene and then wrap for the night," the assistant director pleaded. After considerable thought, and having a degree of sympathy for the predicament everyone was in, I reluctantly called "Action," in a low voice, after which the company wrapped for the night.

The next day, the producers summoned me to a meeting. They said Bill wasn't continuing on the film and they wanted me to take over as director. I said, "Why don't you shut down production for a week and hire a new director?"

These producers had made their money doing low budget erotic thrillers and invested all their profits in this film, which was their first feature. With their $3-million budget stretched to the hilt, they told me they couldn't afford to shut down for even a day.

I told them I was a member of the Directors Guild of America (DGA) and that because their film was a nonunion film that I could get in trouble if I were to take over as director. As a side issue, I wasn't excited about taking over a movie that wasn't my story or my cast.

The producers pleaded with me and said they'd pay any fines and support me with the DGA. In retrospect, I should have called the DGA, but it was exigent circumstances and I felt sorry for these guys. Because I had a great support team on the movie with Tim Gilbert, Richard Epper, and Buck Macdancer as my stunt team, I signed on to finish the movie as the director. This wasn't the way I wanted to begin my directorial career because I didn't like how the picture had been filmed so far, and now all of that part would be attributed to me.

The first night as director, I had a deeply emotional scene in which I directed an actor playing a death row convict who is about to be electrocuted. I was proud of this scene, and the crew saw that I knew what I was doing. James Brolin was fantastic. He could have pitched a fit over the unfolding events but instead helped me, perhaps because as a DGA member, himself, he knew what I was up against.

A year later, Jeff Speakman asked me to do his next film that was being shot in Israel. Again, I signed on as the fight choreographer, stunt coordinator, and second unit director.

During pre-production, Jeff noticed that the movie was mostly action, and since I'd picked up directing on the last film, he recommended to the producers, Avi and Danny Lerner of Millennium films, that I be hired to direct, to which they agreed.

Two weeks later, I was off to Israel to start filming *Deadly Takeover* (aka *Deadly Outbreak*) that had a low budget of $4-million dollars. With all of our limitations, the action movie made money for Millennium Films and was a Showtime and HBO premier event.

To my surprise and, to one degree or another, my disappointment, I found directing to be and an extremely stressful, and often thankless, job. For me, directing is worse than being a cop. No director sets out to make a bad movie. They put their heart and soul in it and do everything they possibly can in the hope of making the best movie possible.

Then when the film is shown, some critic announces to their

Directing Ron Silver in *Deadly Outbreak.*

Directing *Deadly Outbreak.*

millions of followers that the film is a flop. Of course, good reviews
are nothing more than a temporary blessing, as Dustin Hoffman once
pointed out when he said, "A good review from the critics is just another stay of execution."

The sad part is that few critics have any idea about the myriad of
problems that a director faces over the year or two that a film is being made, often overcoming astronomical obstacles with nothing less
than a Herculean effort. In my view, awards should be given based on
the value of the completed film when looked at against all the obstacles and limitations the director faced.

After I finished directing *The Expert* and *Deadly Outbreak*, I had
a monumental ah-ha moment when I learned from those two pictures that the story is far more important than anything. The reason
this hadn't occurred to me prior to directing was because when I
worked as a stuntman and stunt choreographer, all that mattered was
the action.

This was also the case when I worked as a second unit director. Because the scenes I directed, even those that included actors, didn't have dialogue, the story and emotional content were pretty much absent.

The reality that I came to understand is that a director should first tell the story, which I learned from one of Hollywood's most successful director-producers, Sydney Pollock. If the script has a solid story and competent actors, the director doesn't need much of anything else. If two actors are in a room, the director doesn't have to cut away from the room because the audience is captivated by what the actors are doing and saying. Sydney Pollock calls this "the spine," which is similar to the spine of a book. In a sense, the film's story holds the film together in the same manner that a book's spine holds the book together.

This is true because the story is what drives the viewer's emotions, and these emotions have longevity and build as the movie's storyline unfolds. In sharp contrast, this isn't true with a scene depicting a topless dancer or car crash in which the viewer's emotions suddenly peak and then, just as rapidly, flat line.

My friend Ian Quinn invited me to coffee one day. After we chatted for a while, he casually asked if I had any projects that I'd like to direct. In fact, I did. Months earlier, I'd read an intriguing feature article in *Aviation* magazine called "Doolittle's Raiders" and gave Ian their background.

The "Doolittle Raid," also known as the "Tokyo Raid," that occurred on April 18, 1942, was an air raid by the United States on the Japanese capital Tokyo and other places on the island of Honshu during World War II. Because it was the first air raid to strike Japan, it demonstrated that Japan was vulnerable to American air attack, served as retaliation for the Japanese attack on Pearl Harbor four months earlier, and provided an important boost to American morale.

The raid was led by Lieutenant Colonel James "Jimmy"

Doolittle, United States Army Air Forces. Sixteen U.S. B-25B Mitchell medium bombers were launched from the U.S. Navy's aircraft carrier U.S.S. *Hornet* deep in the Western Pacific Ocean, each with a crew of five volunteers, who came from all walks of life.

The plan called for them to bomb military targets in Japan and to continue westward to land in China. Unfortunately, the carrier task force was spotted by a Japanese trawler, and the planes had to take-off 200 miles farther away than planned. As a result, the planes used more fuel and couldn't reach the airfields in China. Fifteen planes ditched along the Chinese coast or crash landed in the mountains, while the 16th landed in the Soviet Union where it was confiscated and its crew interned for more than four years.

Of the 80 Doolittle Raiders, one was killed on bailout and two men drowned when their plane crash landed in water. Of the eight who were captured by the Japanese Army in China, three were executed by firing squad, and one died from beriberi and malnutrition while in prison. Of those who survived, 13 later died after returning to fight in the war.

The article in *Aviation* magazine mentioned that every year the Doolittle survivors come together for a reunion, which I explained to Ian that I'd love to shoot as a documentary. With that, we said our farewells and I went home.

The following day, I received a call from Ian who said, "I got tickets for us to fly to Groton, Connecticut where the Doolittle survivors are having their annual reunion in two weeks at the Air Force Academy." I was instantly ecstatic. Ian had researched the Doolittle Raiders and learned that no one had ever been inside their annual ritualistic private ceremony, although the public was welcome to attend the rest of the reunion.

Apparently, someone at the Discovery Channel had read the same feature article in *Aviation* magazine because one of the station's producers had contacted the spokesperson for the Doolittle survivors

Four members of Doolittle's Raiders (note the case of 80 goblets).

and was trying to put together a deal to cover the reunion. Fortunately, Ian turned out to be a better negotiator, and as a result we were headed to Groton, Connecticut.

Besides being excited and looking forward to directing my first documentary, the filming of the Doolittle survivors' reunion had a special meaning for two reasons. First, all of the 80 men who flew on that mission were around the age of my father, who served in the Navy in WWII. I have no doubt that if he had been asked to volunteer for that mission, he would have proudly accepted.

Secondly, I never felt completely comfortable with my contribution to the military when I served in the Army during the Vietnam War. And so covering the reunion of these brave and honorable men afforded me the opportunity to add a little more to my service to my country.

In April 2005, Ian and I, along with a small crew, flew to Groton, Connecticut to film the week-long 63rd reunion of the

Doolittle Raiders. It was heartwarming to visit with these American heroes, some of whom were infirm and forgetful, but still others who were still in robust physical and mental health (most were in their eighties). Over the week we were there, these men relived their heroic memories, laughed, cried, hugged one another, and shared photos of their wives, children, and grandchildren. I was allowed to interview all of the Raiders and film them, as well as their private ceremony that had never previously been done.

The high point of the reunion was a solemn, private ceremony in which the surviving Raiders performed a roll call, toasting each of their fellow Raiders who had died during the previous year. Specially engraved silver goblets, one for each of the 80 Raiders, were used for this toast.

As the roll was called, the goblets of those who had died were inverted (each Raider's name was engraved on his goblet both right side up and upside down). The Raiders toasted from a bottle of cognac

With members of the Doolittle Raiders.

Donna, producer, and General Doolittle's daughter.

that accompanied the 80 goblets to each reunion. Throughout the year, these goblets are on display at the National Air Force Museum in Dayton, Ohio.

An important part of the reunion ceremony is the opening of a special bottle of 1896 Hennessy Cognac by the last two surviving Raiders (Doolittle was born in 1896). On April 18, 2013, a final reunion for the surviving Raiders was held at Eglin Air Force Base, with Robert Hite being the only survivor unable to attend. The "final toast to fallen comrades" by the surviving raiders took place at the NMUSAF on November 9, 2013, preceded by a B-25 flyover, and was attended by Richard Cole, Edward Saylor, and David Thatcher.

The bartender of that hotel said those old guys drank the bar dry. Remember some of these men in their 80s and 90s were once young war pilots full of spunk. Before our shoot, every day they were up before us exercising or taking long walks—these same men who the night before stayed in the bar telling stories long after I'd gone to bed.

When I did the documentary, I made sure to have a flag ceremony with patriotic music behind it to portray the greatness of these
American soldiers. For as long as I can recall, I've been a diehard
patriot. To this day, when I see a uniformed soldier present a folded
American flag to a widow or a child, I tear up.

As a footnote, years after the documentary was completed, my
Emmy award-winning wife Donna cut it and showed it at a theater in
downtown Los Angeles. In addition, the documentary received honorable mention at the New York Film Festival.

Directing Donna *Hands of Stone.*

Above, working with a second unit camera operator on *Hands of Stone*. Below, directing one of the fight scenes from the same film.

Chapter 16:

Hands of Stone

Although Robert De Niro is a big time Hollywood actor—
many say the best in the history of filmmaking—nominated
seven times for an Academy Award and won twice, he's nothing like the characters he portrays in his movies. People watch him on
a talk show, and he'll just show up and sit down. He hardly has to say
anything but utter one or two words that he accents with his signature
stare and the audience goes wild. To millions of his fans throughout
the world, Robert De Niro is a tough guy who's not to be messed with.
In reality, however, he's far from that.

When Bob is on the set, he's always the same. He has a small
group of people that he requests to be on the film, including his hair-
stylist Jerry Popolis, his makeup artist Carla White, his wardrobe person Monica Ruiz-Ziegler, and I'm his stuntman/double.

Moreover, he always has his director's chair or some type of chair
with a table next to it, and he sits slightly apart from the group. He
likes to be by himself and read a newspaper or talk on his phone or

Me with
Robert De Niro

something similar. Although he's not an aloof person, he appears to be.

Because of his persona, people don't want to go over to him and risk bothering him if they don't have to. Ironically, if someone on the set were to walk over to him and say, "Hi, Bob. I'm curious—what're you reading?" he'd engage with them immediately.

One of several things that Bob and I share in common is that we're both somewhat shy. He's not a man of many words. When he does interviews, he's reserved and at times even appears slightly uncomfortable about talking about himself. I find him to be humble and very much a gentleman.

When I do a stunt for Bob, he sometimes wants to stay on the set to make sure that I do it the way he'd like. Once, I had to fall out of a tree, and he came over and watched and said, "Can you maybe lean this way before you fall? I think I would do that."

I replied, "Sure, Bob" and I did exactly what he requested.

When there's a bulk of time when Bob is told he isn't needed, he goes to his trailer. And yet, he doesn't mind waiting on the set if that's what the director wants. It's important to note that, while I cherish every minute I have with Bob, I've had a limited personal experience of him because I see him only at work.

One would think that because to a certain extent Bob is a method actor, he'd make all the arguments that other actors do. When I've watched him around other big actors, however, he's totally compliant, and often responds, "Sure, I can do that." Whatever the director asks for, Bob can deliver. He's a giving actor who is every director's dream.

My experience of Robert De Niro is that he appears to work best when a competent director tells him exactly what he wants and then gets out of Bob's way and lets the master deliver a prize performance.

In 2012, I was hired to work on the sports comedy *Grudge Match* starring Robert De Niro and Sylvester Stallone as aging boxers stepping into the ring for one last bout. Stallone and De Niro had both previously starred in successful boxing films (*Rocky* and *Raging Bull*, respectively) and worked together on *Cop Land*.

My earliest recollection of watching boxing matches is when I was in high school and my mom bought me a portable 5" Sony TV. I had that TV in my bedroom and watched Eileen Eaton (the mother of Gene LeBell) promote fights at the Olympic Auditorium. These fights were broadcasted over the local channel 5 (KTLA) in Los Angeles, which I was able to pick up in Santa Barbara.

The first fight I watched was Smokin' Joe Frazier, who was a rare boxer with legs the size of tree stumps and would mow down opponents like a freight train. Of course, Frazier is best known for his rock 'em, sock 'em fights with Muhammad Ali. Since high school, I've been enamored with boxing and am a huge fight fan.

To prepare for working on *Grudge Match*, I did some boxing training. Because of my experience as a full contact karate fighter, I knew a little about western boxing, but felt that I didn't know enough. Karate and boxing have different footwork; in fact, they have different everything. First and foremost, I had to get my weight down because Bob was purposely losing weight for his role.

When I began working with Bob on *Killing Season*, my job was to show him how to punch. Mind you, Bob had won an Academy Award for his performance in *Raging Bull* playing boxing legend Jake La Motta, and the majority of those scenes were done by Bob, not a double.

So he knew a little bit about fighting. But the stunt coordinator, Jeff Imada, wanted me to "work with your actor," and so I did. I just kept saying, "Well, Bob, you probably don't need it. Ah, that's good, Bob, I know you've done this before."

He'd smile and say, "Oh great."

I met with Sylvester Stallone's trainer, Bob Salley, and together we went over the movie's fight sequences. Because of De Niro's past experience, he ended up doing all the fighting on *Grudge Match*, and I doubled him doing other stunts.

While the movie was being filmed, I got on a workout routine and picked up the boxing basics—the footwork and the body movement of slipping and sliding, and combination work and how to throw a proper jab and a proper hook—all those things came to fruition.

Above, JT, his double, Jeff Imada, Robert De Niro and me doubling for him on *Killing Season*. On right, I am doubling in that film (notice the camera operator on the bottom).

Doubling Bob.

Because of my previous knowledge of fighting, these things came quickly for me.

During the shoot, director Jonathan Jakubowicz arrived on the set. Jonathan has an interesting background. Born in Caracas, Venezuela in 2005, he jumped to international film recognition after he wrote, directed, and produced the action thriller *Secuestro Express* that became Venezuela's highest-grossing film. I soon learned that he was set to direct Bob in Jonathan's next movie *Hands of Stone*, which is a boxing movie centered on the life of legend Roberto Duran.

Roberto Duran Samaniego is widely regarded as one of the

greatest boxers of all time. A versatile brawler in the ring, he was nick-named *"Manos de Piedra"* ("Hands of Stone") during his career. In 2002, Duran was voted by *The Ring* magazine as the fifth greatest fighter of the last 80 years, while boxing historian Bert Sugar rated him as the eighth greatest fighter of all time. In June 1980, Duran defeated Sugar Ray Leonard to capture the WBC welterweight title but shocked the boxing world by returning to his corner in the November rematch, saying *"no mas"* ("no more"). This is a prime example that even the most ferocious fighters in the world can have a night when they are the exception of "no quit."

Jonathan Jakubowicz had come to the *Grudge Match* set because he wanted to see how boxing sequences were filmed. After we wrapped the film, several months went by, and then one morning my phone rang. It was Johnathan and one of the producers, Jay Weisleder, calling to say that he wanted to hire me as stunt coordinator on *Hands of Stone*, which he described as a little boxing movie to be filmed in Panama. I was in, if for no other reason than Bob had been cast in the movie.

I'd never been to Panama, whose entire economy and political clout comes from its sole ownership of the Panama Canal, which is

Donna and I arrive in Panama.

a 48-mile ship canal that connects the Atlantic Ocean to the Pacific Ocean. So Donna and I packed up to go.

The crew was 100 percent South American, and most had never made a movie before, except for the Mexican grips and electricians. To further complicate matters, upon my arrival, I learned that the movie had huge battle scenes related to the Civil War of Panama, and all I brought with me were three stunt people, no equipment, no air

With Roberto Duran and son Chavo.

bags, nothing—and only minimal special effects were supplied from Mexico.

My experience on *Hands of Stone* was deeply moving because members of the Duran family were involved. Panama is a boxing country that boasts 38 world champions. In the city's main square is an enormous bronze statue of Roberto Duran, who is in real life a hero to millions of Panamanians. Duran's sons were involved in the making of the movie because they were hired to train actor Edgar

Ramirez, who played the role of Duran and didn't know how to box—not even how to stand or throw a jab.

When I arrived, Duran's sons, Chavo and Robin, had been training Edgar in Roberto's son's gym, which was a modern gym that didn't have a boxing feel to it. I watched Edgar's training, and while I thought it was good, I felt that we needed to step up the pace. In order to accomplish this, I moved to a gym called Los Rockeros, which is

Entrance to Los Rockeros.

in one of Panama's many ghettos. This boxing gym is housed on the fourth floor of a five-story ramshackle building.

When I entered the first floor with my boxing gear and three stuntmen, it looked like a criminal front. Although I was told it was a furniture store, throughout the several months I was there, I never saw anybody walk in and buy anything. It was creepy, and many of the men sitting around gave me creepy looks.

As we left the air conditioned first floor, we could feel the second

The Los
Rockeros gym
was *perfect*.

floor warm immediately, as the a/c struggled. The second floor was filled with furniture. The third and fourth floors were cluttered with old, rusted workout equipment, including bicycles and weights, and a hodgepodge of assorted junk. The broken heavy bags thrown in a corner looked like they hadn't been touched in years. Off to one side was a couch, its cushions piled high with dust-covered boxing gloves.

All three floors above the ground floor weren't air conditioned, and with each floor the temperature got hotter because in Panama the temperature is almost always 98 degrees with 98 percent humidity. I was pouring sweat from just breathing.

As we climbed to the fourth floor, I heard the sound of a boxing gym — jump roping, bags getting hit, a rhythmic clatter of a speed bag. Entering the vast room, I saw hand wraps hanging on the windows (there was no glass, just iron bars) being aired out. Hanging from the ceiling, which was corrugated aluminum sheeting that sounded like machine gun fire when it rained, were rows of gloves and headgear that were also airing out.

In the center of the room was an old boxing ring surrounded by sagging ropes and a canvas that had a large crease in the middle. There were holes in the floor and the plumbing was half-broken. There was no place to sit except one broken chair behind the desk where Tolete, the man who ran the gym, sat. The stale air reeked of body sweat.

I walked into the gym and said to Edgar, "This place has the feel. It's going to give you a strong sense of what boxing is about. This has Roberto Duran written all over it."

I introduced Edgar to Tolete, and the two started training. Edgar was a fast learner, and after a half hour said, "This is where we're coming from now on."

Training with Tolete.

David Arosemena,
who played a
young Roberto
Duran.

I was pleased that he liked the gym and added, "We'll still bring Duran's guys in to help with your teaching. Every morning we'll work on fight choreography in the hotel and in the afternoon you come here and train. Just like you're a boxer. And you have to diet like a boxer."

It turned out that my main job was to choreograph many of Duran's 119 professional fights, including Duran's fights with boxing legend Sugar Ray Leonard. Because of this detailed choreography, *Hands of Stone* is the most accurate boxing film in movie history because every fight seen on the screen is exactly as Duran's real fights played out. I duplicated every feint, every duck, every punch, every slip, and every jab and mirrored these in my actors. I directed part of the fight sequences, as did Jonathan Jakubowicz.

At the end of our training regime, actor Edgar Ramirez looked like Roberto Duran. We did the same thing with the international R&B pop music superstar Usher, who plays Sugar Ray Leonard. Few would have

Left, training Usher. Below, playing a real scene with Bob as Gil Clancy.

ever, in their wildest imagination, guessed that Usher could have been believable as Sugar Ray Leonard. And yet, the people who have viewed Usher's fight footage have remarked, "Ohmygod, really?!" I played the part of Hall of Fame boxing trainer Gil Clancy.

Without question, *Hands of Stone* has Oscar potential. Robert De Niro plays Duran's manager, Ray Arcel, who coached Roberto Duran and was an active boxing trainer from the 1920s through the 1980s and trained 18 world champions. As only Bob could do, he emulated Arcel's hair, aged look, and body mannerisms.

With Edgar Ramirez.

In addition to an all-star cast and an extraordinarily gifted director, cinematically the film is in a league all its own. Director of photography Miguel Ioann Littin Menz is a cinematic master. Every shot is a mural and Academy Award worthy.

At the end of the film when I did my "behind the scenes" interview, I had such an emotional high that I broke down and cried because my heart and soul had become attached to the Los Rockeros gym, Tolete, Maria Toto—and everyone associated with this four-month film shoot.

Above, my fantastic *Hands of Stone* team. on the right, with Ruben Blades, who played Roberto Duran's promoter Carlos Eleta.

The majority of the hundreds of hours I spent working on *Hands of Stone* were spent getting Edgar Ramirez up to speed to play the part of Robert Duran and Usher up to speed in his choreography to fight Edgar as Sugar Ray Leonard. With my own history as a fighter, I became so entrenched in the training gym in the Rockeros ghetto that I began training with Tolete and routinely sparring with some of the amateurs.

In addition, my own training regime included combination work on mitts, footwork, heavy bag, and speed bag work. At the end of four months, I'd reached the level of an amateur boxer, and yet had no idea where that might lead—although I was about to find out.

Chapter 17:

USA Masters Boxing

Having been a fighter for more than four decades, I've learned several significant differences between martial arts fighting and boxers. The biggest difference is that boxers find out how they react to getting hit hard or when they throw everything they have at their opponent and it has no effect.

I see this in the boxing gym at least twice a month. A new guy will come into the gym to test the waters. Unfortunately, the rite of passage in most boxing gyms is that the new person will be handed a pair of boxing gloves and put in a ring where he will get his butt beat by a skilled boxer. This new guy is then told that if he's got the heart, he'll come back and the gym's trainers will teach him. While this instantly weeds out most new people to boxing who in all likelihood wouldn't last three months, I personally don't agree with this method.

When I was a kid, my cousin Frankie and I found some boxing gloves and threw them on without even lacing them. We boxed around a little, trying to be like Rocky Marciano or whoever the heavyweight boxing champ was at the time, when out of nowhere Frankie hit me square in the nose. Instantly, my eyes flooded with tears, as a lightning bolt of hurt shot into my brain. That was enough for me. I didn't want to do that anymore. I've never forgotten the reality of that moment thinking to myself, *Wow, this hurts!*

Boxing (including kickboxing) and mixed martial arts (MMA) are arguably the most courageous of all spectator sports. What other sport has two individuals run the risk of being totally humiliated in

front of thousands—sometimes millions—of spectators watching for their own entertainment? No one escapes this. Even the best boxers and MMA fighters have been knocked down, knocked out, or choked out. I'm extraordinarily impressed by these fighters who allow them-selves to be tested in front of the public, risking total failure, and they do this practically naked.

When I was a kid, my fear about moving on to high school and getting beat up had nothing to do with a fear of being physically hurt. The fear I had was a fear of being embarrassed as the result of get-ting my ass kicked. Nothing is worse to a kid than to be laughed at, made fun of, and even felt sorry for. I would much rather break a few bones and bleed all over the sidewalk if the end result was that I was declared the winner. For me, this was compounded because I already had a fair degree of feeling inadequate, and losing a fight would most assuredly have added to that.

The only thing that will keep a fighter from being embarrassed is showing tremendous courage. Martial arts kickboxing champion Joe Lewis's last fight showed phenomenal courage. In the movies, the best example I've seen of raw courage was in *Raging Bull* when Sugar Ray Robinson beat the daylights out of Jake La Motta (played by Robert De Niro), who was hurt so badly at the end of the fight that he could hardly see or walk. But he managed to go over to Robinson's corner, and sporting swollen eyes that were mere slits and a mask of blood, he said, "You didn't knock me down, Ray. You didn't knock me down." That was Jake La Motta telling Ray Robinson that he didn't have quit in him, and right up to the end of the fight, La Motta took everything that Ray had and left it in the ring. This is what Coach Mangus taught me when I lost my wrestling matches in high school—that even if I lost a fight, as long as I showed no quit, I was a winner. This is how fighters who lose matches gain respect.

When it comes to extreme mental and physical preparation, I've found that, generally speaking, training in boxing is far superior to training in martial arts. Martial arts training has its advantage, however. I believe that when taught by a competent karate instructor, martial arts training develops a better all-around character. Never has this been better stated than by Gichin Funakoshi, who said, "The ultimate aim in karate lies not in victory or defeat, but in the perfection of the character of its participants."

Ironically, most martial arts are dangerously misleading because the student is taught how to fight, defend, maim, and even kill, but in reality what they learn will rarely happen the way it does in their school. Unlike martial arts students, beginning boxers know immediately what a real fight is about. There's no game playing boun-cy-bouncy tag that martial arts point fighters do while wearing protec-tive equipment to insure they don't get hurt.

Unfortunately, many martial artists freeze when faced with a real street confrontation or discover that much of what they were taught is tragically ineffective. Heavyweight boxing champion Mike Tyson put it simply when he said, "Everyone has a plan until they get punched in the mouth."

Boxing puts an individual into instant combat, albeit with rules.

Rick sparring.

The first awareness that a person learns in the street or the boxing ring is that there is a person who isn't throwing punches slowly and pre-dictably, but instead is throwing fast, erratic punches with the intent of doing major bodily harm.

If a person has never been exposed to this type of assault, it will immediately overwhelm them. Their adrenalin will take over, and the result will be that they won't think clearly and will quickly gas out. Although in martial arts schools an assault is simulated through training, the assault isn't reality based the way it is in MMA schools and boxing gyms.

When I began boxing, the first thing I noticed was that I had to overcome an anxiousness in me that was caused by my opponent. Another descriptive word would be trepidation. Feeling this way is common to practically everyone who is new to boxing. One veteran boxer explained this from the perspective of my opponent. "He's afraid of you because he doesn't know you. Now, you mustn't feel that fear like he does. You must make him realize with your first punch that he has good reason to be feeling the way he does."

As I mentioned earlier, this trepidation is actually my worrying that I won't perform to the best of my ability, lose the fight, and be

humiliated in front of the spectators. What I've learned over the years is that the best way to cancel or counteract this trepidation is to step into the ring knowing that my training has resulted in my being the best boxer I can be. A fighter who brings this mindset to a fight will win every time.

A good boxer, wrestler, or MMA fighter knows this. When I've fought, I've needed to control my breathing, my emotions, my adrenalin, and most of all my thoughts. At all costs, I must remain positive and self-ego driven that I will either dominate my opponent or die.

In many ways, the boxing ring imitates life, itself. How will I react to someone repeatedly hitting me as hard as they can? Will I get wild and just retaliate or be calm, use my footwork, use the technique I've honed in sparring? Will I quit? Will I throw my hands over my head and scream, "I give!" To most people new to boxing, it's easy to quit when they're losing. But a true warrior has to die first, to get choked out or knocked out. True warriors give their all.

This also applies to a movie stunt that has an element of being life-threatening. There have been times when the director says action, and the thought flashes through my mind, *I don't know why I am here*. But because I'm ego-driven, I jump off that five-story building, anyway.

๑ ๑ ๑

While I was in Panama working on the movie *Hands of Stone*, the training camp on that picture turned me into a respectable boxer. After the film wrapped and I'd been home for several weeks, I received a call from professional photographer Manny Fernandez, who wanted to meet with me to shoot a series of boxing photos for a piece he was posting on the Internet.

Manny and I met at Nelson's gym in North Hollywood where I put on a robe and gloves and stepped into the ring. After the photo-shoot, Manny showed me samples of his work that included photos of older, graying boxers. These gentlemen were wearing robes and gloves just like I'd worn for the shoot.

"These guys former champions?" I asked.

"They're not former," Manny replied. "They're still boxing."

"Really?"

"Indeed. They belong to Masters Boxing. Most are in their forties and fifties, but some are in their seventies."

"How active are they?" I said.

"They do it all—sparring, training, competition."

"What sort of competition?" I asked, growing interested.

"These guys fight in the ring. Their fights are sanctioned by USA Boxing—the same people who do Golden Gloves for the Olympics."

"No kidding. Can I get in this?"

"Sure. You just have to pass a physical. If you pass, USA Boxing will issue you a passbook and you're good to go."

I soon discovered that Masters Boxing is a growing sport that's attracting thousands of participants. Some are white collar workers who want to try their hand at boxing, while others are former amateur athletes.

I wasted no time. A week later, doctors signed off on my eyes and general health. All that remained was a stress test, which pleased my wife, who occasionally asked me what would happen if I had a heart attack while flying. To satisfy us both, we went to Santa Barbara to have the test done. After I ran on a sophisticated treadmill for three minutes, the doctor looked over the numbers and said, "You've passed. Do you want to go further and see how you compare to others?"

Sparring partner Ronald Minera.

"Sure," I said.

He gradually increased the angle of the ramp and speed of the treadmill. I ran faster and faster, and after a while had to hold onto a bar, which caused my forearms to tire, even though I wasn't winded. After I'd run for another few minutes, I asked, "So where am I now?"

The doctor glanced at the monitor. "If you can go for another two minutes, you'll be in the 99 percentile of the healthiest hearts in the United States."

Wow. I had no idea I was that healthy. I stayed with it for another minute, and then I couldn't hold onto the bar any longer. I turned to Donna and smiled. "Honey, is this good enough for you? Are you satisfied I won't keel over while flying?"

Donna smiled back. "It's good enough for me."

While I waited for my sanctioning from USA Boxing, I started training at Nelson's Gym, which has since changed its name to Superb Boxing. I had Ronald Minera as a sparring partner, and the gym's owner, Jose Miranda, as my coach.

With Freddy Roach and Paul Mayorquin.

Rick vs. Mike Smith.

When they got me up to speed, we had a difficult time finding a fight in the Masters Boxing ranks because the rules stated that I could only fight another boxer who was within ten pounds of my weight and ten years of my age. Eventually we found a fight with Old Dog Boxing, which is an organization that each year sponsors five boxing events that are held at South Coast Martial Arts in Costa Mesa.

Mike Smith had three inches over me in height, weighed a few pounds heavier, and had four fights under his belt to my zero. I didn't care about Mike's advantage because I'd worked hard, even though I had no idea of what hard was to these guys.

When fight night arrived, Mike Smith and I fought three two-minute rounds, which is standard in the Masters ranking at the time. Although I was certain I'd won the first round, when the bell rang for round two, I was worried about getting gassed.

Boxing is an extremely cardiovascular sport. People who have never been in the ring have no concept of what it's like to get gassed. They'll comment, "Why is that fighter backing away and slowing down?"

My response to those who ask this is, "You get in that ring and

With Ray Boom Boom Mancini .

try throwing rapid punches for all you're worth for a full minute. Go ahead, and you'll see the problem." If they don't want to get in the ring against an opponent, I tell them to just punch air as hard and as fast as they can for a full minute, and the result will be the same.

When a boxer gets gassed, they're so tired that they can't get air into their lungs. I remember reading about Bruce Lee's fight with the highly-skilled kung-fu practitioner Wong Jack Man. At the end of the fight, which lasted much longer than Bruce had anticipated, Bruce realized that his cardio had failed him miserably. Since the day I read that accounting, I've never allowed my cardiovascular system to become substandard.

In my Masters Boxing fight against Mike Smith, when the bell rang for the second round, I was worried from a strategic standpoint that if I worked as hard in the second round as I did in the first round, I might not last to the end of the fight. I wasn't afraid of getting hurt or even knocked out. I just didn't want to be embarrassed from losing the fight because it was obvious that I'd run out of gas. Even though I pulled back in the second round, the round was scored even. In round three, Mike Smith edged me out on points and ended up winning the fight fair and square.

After my first fight, I knew I hadn't given 1,000 percent and was determined to work twice as hard for my next opportunity. Kobe Bryant once said that if a person prepares beyond what their opponents are doing, then they already won. I knew that in my division that no one was working as hard as I was because Donna and I had living with us a professional boxer whose training routine was much lighter than mine.

My revised regime consisted of an hour every morning of cardiovascular and weightlifting, followed by ten rounds of heavy bag, speed bag, jump rope, elastic bag, and head movement. Additionally, three nights a week, I sparred six to eight rounds with sparring partners who were always younger and heavier.

When I returned to my next Old Dog Boxing event at South

With Tommy "Hit Man" Hearns and Eddie Murphy from *Beverly Hills Cop 2*.

Coast Martial Arts, I was no longer worried about getting gassed—and I didn't care who my opponent was because there was no way he was going to win.

My new training regime paid high dividends. Again, the fight was scheduled for three rounds. The first two rounds, my opponent was forced to take two standing eight counts, and at the end of the fight, I was awarded the match by unanimous decision. I hit him so hard, when I called the guy the next day I felt bad because he said he still had a headache from our match.

Infused with that winning feeling, I decided to take the next step and compete in the USA Boxing Nationals competition that were to be held in Lenexa, Kansas. This competition was a whole other deal because I had to make weight at 152 pounds, which meant I had to diet. Often boxers who drop in weight pay the price of losing power. I was adamant this wasn't going to happen. In fact, I structured my training routine so that I would be even more powerful at this lower weight. I was going to leave nothing in the gym and knock my opponent out. I was going to hit him so hard that the wax would fly out of his ears!

I timed my training so that three days before the fight, I was peaked out. My weight and cardio were perfect. I was ready because I knew that my opponent wasn't sparring as much and as hard as I was because he probably doesn't love it as much as I do.

The nationals is bigger because people come from all over the world. I flew to Lenexa, Kansas and eventually stared across the ring at my opponent, who was a big Texan. I say big because the problem in my division is that I'm only 5'7" and the other fighters are 5'10" and above—so I always give up that substantial height advantage.

As the fight progressed, it was a repeat of my last fight. By the end of round two, my opponent had taken two standing eight counts. By the start of round three, I knew I had a big advantage because I saw his jaw had dropped and that he was out of air. When I hit him, his head would go askew and he was moving to get away from me. Near the end of the fight, I went after him, determined to knock him out. But he was strong, and I respected him for having no quit. It didn't matter, however, and I was awarded the fight and, as a result won the National Championship, as well as accepting a sponsorship from Title Boxing, for which I was both happy and grateful.

My next step was that I decided to go to the 2015 USA Masters Boxing World Championships that were held in Kansas City, Kansas. The annual World Championships are the grand finale of USA Masters Boxing. Each year, thousands of people from throughout the world travel to attend this spectacular full week of competition.

As I had been in my previous fights, I was totally convinced that no fighter my approximate size and age could beat me—both mentally, which is the most powerful aspect of fighting, or physically. I

Winning the World Title.

simply was not going to be denied. I arrived at the world championships with a steadfast mindset and no quit—and won the USA Masters
Boxing World Title.

Chapter 18:

Goin' Home

When last year I worked in New York with Robert De Niro on *The Intern*, on my day off I took the train to East Bronx because I wanted to see if anything had changed. Even though I spent only my first 13 years there, those years were my initial lifetime experience. While on the train, I reflected on my life as I gazed out the window at the passing sights and listened to the clatter of the train wheels rolling along the tracks.

I'm at a place in my life where I'm comfortable around my peers when I go to work. I can go on any movie set anywhere in the world and there're enough people on that set who know me, and some gray-haired person who says, "Hey, Rick!" I'm comfortable with whatever airport I'm in, any country I visit, and any cop or black belt I meet. I've reached a comfort zone that comes with age and has a feeling of belonging that for me is enough.

Occasionally in my adult life, I've thought about that rainy night in Santa Barbara when I had a chance meeting with John Travolta.

I could have been off that night, or looked for his Jag on another street, or had a flat tire, or written a standard incident report and driven away. But none of that happened. It was almost as if meeting the most famous movie star in the early 1980s, and under those unique circumstances, etched my fate in stone. Even prior to meeting John Travolta, had I not purchased the karate school, I would never have

The Taurus Award.

gotten into police work or met Kim Kahana or Hal Needham or Alan Gibbs.

With the exception of memorizing Morse code, I wasn't blessed with an exceptional God-given talent. Yet because of that chance meeting one rainy night in Santa Barbara, coupled with a few key mentors who were unselfishly willing to invest their time and interest in me, I've done exceptionally well in life.

There're great stuntmen with lots more talent than I have. But because of the mentoring I received from Alan Gibbs, I've been confident that any production company can take me on a location and I'll get the fire gag done. I can hop on the motorcycle or a horse; I can get the car gag done; I can do all the journeyman arts of the trade—everything from falling down a flight of stairs to doing huge car jumps and rollovers.

To my knowledge, I'm the only man in the world who has a widely diversified and extensive resume for flying helicopters, followed by a martial arts resume, and a lengthy stunt resume. As a final triumph in the stunt world, I received the coveted Taurus Award for "Best

Vehicular Work" for *The Dark Knight*, as well as two SAG awards and a third nomination.

I've sometimes wondered what my life would have been like had I taken a civil service job like that of a postal worker. I'd go to work, enjoy my limited clientele whom I saw every week. I'd put in my hours with few worries and go home at night having left my job at the post office. And then the next day, do it all over again—day after day, week after week, month after month, year after year, and then retire with a comfortable pension.

While there is something to be said about that type of job, it's never been for me because I need continual change in my life. Just as important, I need life to be unpredictable, challenging, and include the element of risk.

When the train arrived in East Bronx, I got off about two miles from my old house and began walking. Fifteen minutes later, I came upon PS 97 where I attended school in my adolescence. Aside from cosmetic maintenance, the school remained unchanged. The playground had the same backboard for dodgeball and handball, and the tetherball poles and chain-link fencing looked unchanged. When I walked along the hallways of the main building that housed the classrooms, the place smelled the same. Even the water from the child's-height porcelain drinking fountain had a familiar taste.

At one point, I came upon the very spot that Billy Kowalski often threatened to punch me in my arm if I didn't hand over my lunch money. The memory triggered a wave of mixed emotions. I felt sorry that Billy had died in prison and wished he could have seen that I was no longer little Ricky—the weak, timid kid who was afraid to go to Columbus High School, and yet now is considered a close friend and equal to some of the most macho stuntmen in Hollywood and recently won the USA Masters Boxing World Championship. I wondered if Billy would have been proud of me.

Had I really accomplished that much? I sat down on a nearby

bench and recalled the afternoon in 1997 when I was walking off the lot at Paramount Studios and saw far in the distance the famous "Hollywood" sign displayed just below the top of Mount Lee. I'd just landed the job of stunt coordinator on *Star Trek: Insurrection*, and even carried the script in my hand. There I was looking at that famous Hollywood sign, and I'm on the lot of one of the biggest movie studios in Hollywood and I thought *Wow, I'm doing a Star Trek movie that I used to watch when I was a kid! Wow! Who would have ever predicted this?*

While I've taken in stride my share of bumps in the road, my one regret is the failing of my marriages to Sue and Joni. If I'd done a better job, my children, who were young at the time those marriages ended, wouldn't have paid such a heavy price.

I got up from the bench and began walking toward my old house that was a little over a mile away. I was amazed by how everything seemed so familiar. Many of the buildings had been remodeled and

Coordinating *Star Trek.*

some had even been torn down. Most familiar of all were the young kids playing in their four-square-block neighborhood that for a while would be their entire world.

A half-block later, I found myself thinking about my mom and remembered the words of Meryl Streep, who said, "You don't have to be famous. You just have to make your mother and father proud of you." I often reflected on how my mother hated that I left Cal Poly. When I began my stunt career, I'd sometimes come home on weekends and she'd ask what I was doing. I never wanted to tell her until I was leaving because I knew she still wasn't happy that I didn't finish college.

Even though I was making an excellent living as a stuntman, to my mom, if I wasn't a doctor or a lawyer, it didn't matter how much money I made. Perhaps I was only imagining this because I later heard stories about how after I left she'd be playing Mahjong or cards with her friends and all she could talk about was her son Ricky and his Hollywood stunt work. I think as she got older, she realized that the amount of education I went through to learn my craft as a stuntman, along with the hundreds of hours I spent becoming a licensed pilot and flight instructor, were comparable to a four or six year college degree.

As I drew closer to my old house, I passed by the corner building that used to be Nat's Italian Deli and is now "Casa Doro Delicatessen." It suddenly seemed like yesterday that, as an eight-year-old kid, I walked into Nat's to buy a six-pack of Schlitz beer for my dad.

The memory made me think about something actor Ray Romano once said. There was a time when he was the highest paid actor in television, earning over a million dollars per episode for *Everybody Loves Raymond*. The day following Raymond's appearance on David Letterman's final show, he said during an interview, "I go out on stage to get some kind of approval from an audience because I never got it when I was growing up. I've always said that if my father had even hugged me just once I'd probably be an accountant today. Without that angst there wouldn't be any show business. Our only entertainment would be bowling."

Reflecting back on my relationship with my father, I can relate to those words. Had my dad lived, I think that eventually we would have jelled. I think it would be great to be spending time and doing things together. I sometimes feel sad that I can't sit with him and talk with him about my career in Hollywood and its worth, and that he couldn't have gone along on the ride. I think he would have loved coming to a set.

To say that I'm extremely proud of my own children would be a vast understatement. Dianne became a deputy sheriff and worked for the Los Angeles Sheriffs' Department from 1998 to 2002. Unfortunately, a back injury forced her to retire, which broke her heart. In 2010, she would bless us with a grandson, Cody, with her former

I pin badge on my daughter when she becomes a Deputy Sheriff.

Above, Brian playing high school football. On left, Brian doing a rollover.

deputy husband Arin Cinocco. Today, she continues with her college studies and is an online program coordinator for three public charter schools in Los Angeles.

In 1994, Brian started his stunt career and has over 250 movie and TV credits. Highly skilled, he is regarded by his peers as a go-to stuntman they can rely on.

Brian and his wife Lisa have blessed me with two beautiful grand-daughters, Mia and Meegan, born in 2008 on Christmas day and July 22, 2011, respectively.

Top left, Mikey appearing on *Baywatch*; top right, a group portrait, clockwise from top: Mia, Meegan. Bailey, and Cody - with Mikey in the middle. On the left, hockey goalie Mikey.

Mikey is living a healthy life, has recently completed a triathlon, and was a member of the ski patrol here in Southern California after leaving the stunt business with 25 years under his belt. He presently donates his services to "Riding on Insulin," which is an organization that helps young diabetics. The happiest contribution to our family is a beautiful granddaughter named Bailey.

Above, Mikey with ski dog; below, with my sons Brian and Mikey.

Above, with Donna and Gary; below, me and Donna.

When I came upon the Morgan Avenue street sign, much to my amazement, tears suddenly filled my eyes. At the time, I had no idea what had caused this surge of emotion. I brushed them away, made the right hand turn, and walked toward my old house. The trees were the same, as were the cracks in the concrete that hadn't been repaired in all these years.

Suddenly, I was there at 2506 Morgan Avenue. Except for a new coat of paint and a half dozen new windows, the old brownstone was the same. At that moment, I recognized the smell of the air that was distinctly "my neighborhood" and vividly remembered what it was like as a child waking up in the morning to that fresh air coming through my bedroom window and that wonderful feeling of being a child and eagerly facing a new day. Ironically, I even recalled our old phone number.

My tears returned, but this time more profound as I suddenly found myself standing in front of my old house, sobbing. Then it occurred to me—what I was feeling was the age old wonderment of "coming home." At that moment, I truly missed the easy life and felt blessed that I'd lived during a more pleasant, simpler time. My childhood was during an era that only those who grew up during the '50s and '60s—when we went from AM radio to the moon—will truly understand.

Now the sun had set and the sky was beginning to darken. Just then, a block away, a streetlight came on. Moments later, a second, and then a third. From afar, I heard a woman calling out, her voice sounding like that of a mother calling her children. The woman's voice was echoed by another, this time closer, and then another. And then, what sounded as if it were coming from the top of my porch, I heard the sound of my mother's voice calling, "Ricky! Dinner! Ricky, c'mon!! Dinner's on the table!"

I looked up and smiled. I didn't have to come running on this particular evening, for I was already home.

ᔥ ᔥ ᔥ

I am the son of many fathers. My dad Edward "Sonny" left me at an early age. Fred, Nat, and Coach Mangus all had a hand in my upbringing. Scott Mitchell, Joe Lewis, and Alan Gibbs developed me from there. Some are gone, as well as my cherished mother and sister Kim. To them I refer to this poem for comfort:

> Do not stand at my grave and weep.
> I am not there; I do not sleep.
> I am a thousand winds that blow.
> I am the diamond glints on snow.
> I am the sunlight on ripened grain.
> I am the gentle autumn rain.
> When you awaken in the morning's hush
> I am the swift uplifting rush
> Of quiet birds in circled flight.
> I am the soft star that shines at night.
> Do not stand at my grave and cry;
> I am not there; I did not die.
> —Mary Elizabeth Frye

Please visit the following websites related to Rick Avery:

WWW.RICKAVERY.NET
(Rick can be contacted through this site)

WWW.4BLADEHELICOPTERS.COM

WWW.HARDKNOCKS.TV

WWW.ISASTUNTS.COM

WWW.LAMSPORTS.COM

Tom Bleecker

began his writing career in 1969 as a screenwriter for director Blake Edwards. After nearly two decades writing for screen and television, in 1987 Bleecker co-authored his first book with Linda Lee, *The Bruce Lee Story*, which served as the source material for MCA Universal's motion picture *Dragon*. In 1996, Bleecker wrote a second book on Lee, a highly controversial bestseller entitled *Unsettled Matters*. After penning nearly 50 biographies, in 2012 Bleecker wrote his first novel *Tea Money*. Prior to *A Life at Risk*, Bleecker's last two biographies were (in 2014) *The Jet* (the life story of kickboxing legend Benny "The Jet" Urquidez) and (in 2015) *My Song* (the life story of New York socialite Jolanta Soysal). He and his wife, Lourdes, live in Southern California. The author can be contacted through his website www.tombleecker.com.